LEGI✝ DISCIPLE

The Extraordinary Work of the Holy Spirit in You

MARY AMESBURY

Mary Amesbury

Wasteland Press

www.wastelandpress.net
Shelbyville, KY USA

Legit Disciple: The Extraordinary Work of the Holy Spirit in You
By Mary Amesbury

First printing – January 2014
ISBN: 978-1-60047-938-0

Printed in the U.S.A.

0   1   2   3   4   5   6   7   8

Dedicated to Bob and Astrida Kuhns, who were my visual aids of the abundant life in Christ. Your love, patient teaching, and never-ending encouragement brought me to a place of freedom in Christ. You taught me how to walk by the Holy Spirit and find satisfaction in Christ. Without you, this book would never have been possible. I can never thank you enough for what your lives have meant to me. You have been the fragrance of Christ to me.

"The thief does not come except to steal, and to kill, and to destroy. I have come that they may have life, and that they may have it more abundantly" (John 10:10).

TABLE OF CONTENTS

SECTION ONE: *The Holy Spirit*

SECTION TWO: *Freedom in Christ*

SECTION ONE:
The Holy Spirit

1

Introduction

God's design for *every* believer is that he or she would be holy – both morally victorious and free to follow Jesus without hindrance. This is not, however, one of those guilt-inducing books that sets an impossibly high standard for believers and then declares that "if you really love Jesus" you'll just do what you are supposed to do. This book comes from the perspective of someone who really does love Jesus but who didn't have a clue how to be a legit Christian on the inside.

Our Christian life is meant to be a satisfying experience that brings delight to both God and His children. But the practice of that often falls short of the reality, because we are unaware of the ordinary (but really extraordinary) ministries of the Holy Spirit in the lives of believers.

It is the Spirit who makes us legit disciples by transforming us from sinner to saint through giving us victory over sin and by crafting a new

> *It is the Spirit who makes us legit disciples by transforming us from sinner to saint through giving us victory over sin and by crafting a new character in our soul.*

character in our soul. It is the Holy Spirit who is God's exquisite gift to us that makes us able to live a godly Christian life. In this book, we will discover what the Holy Spirit is doing in the lives of every Christian every day. The hope is that as you realize all that you have, you will find greater satisfaction in Jesus Christ than you have ever experienced before.

Having come to Christ for salvation after college, I initially grew rapidly. Sinful ways of thinking and acting were transformed and I became truly different than who I'd been as an unsaved person. I loved reading the Bible and hearing it preached. A year and a half after giving my life to Jesus, I was in seminary preparing for full-time Christian service. I earned my Masters in Biblical Studies in three years. Six and a half years after my salvation, I was part of a group of pioneer missionaries under Baptist Mid-Missions beginning a church in the Russian Far East. It was the fast track, and it was exciting. For the most part, I was so over my head that I was dependent on the Lord on a daily basis as I attempted to do ministry in an unfamiliar culture and language.

But when my health broke down and I was forced to come back to the United States and change my ministry to Campus Bible Fellowship International, a subtle shift began to take over. Here in the States I didn't have a language or culture that would require being overly dependent on the Lord. The foundation I had built for my Christian walk was DIY – do-it-yourself. I felt that it was my responsibility to produce Christian character in myself (and others). It was my responsibility to measure up to what I thought were God's standards. I used guilt to motivate myself and the students to whom I was ministering.

I became more focused on matching up with the unwritten standard of what was "spiritual" in the eyes of my fellow churchgoers and less focused on Christ Himself. My Christian walk was energized by a fear of failure rather than a joy in my relationship with Jesus.

Church services often felt boring, and there was little true worship going on in my heart. Of course, the "big" sins had no part in my life. But the sins of the heart like envy, jealousy, judgmentalism, complaining, fear, and worry were rampant. Emotionally, I was all over the map. To be honest, I didn't feel like a legit Christian – I felt like a loser. Sometimes the Christian life just seemed like bondage to "always trying to measure up." I feared failure. I was frustrated by my own inability to have victory over sin and genuine Christian character. I longed for a more fulfilling relationship with Jesus Christ and His church. I was constantly looking for *the* book or program or idea that would make it all work.

You can gasp and judge if you want, but the reality is that most of us, I suspect, are doing the Christian walk more often in the flesh than we'd like to admit. We just don't know any other way.

I knew that Jesus must have intended something more for His followers. In Acts 17:6 the testimony concerning the first century church was that they had *"turned the world upside down."* Obviously, they had something more than what I was experiencing. And yet I also knew that God doesn't have different levels of Christians – some who get a bigger dose of spirituality than the run-of-the-mill Christians who are supposed to be content with barely getting by.

A couple of years after returning to the United States, I read a book filled with the testimonies of Christians who had fulfilling, useful, productive Christian lives and victory over sin. For weeks I studied the Scriptures to prove whether what was outlined in the book was true. I enthusiastically shared my new theories and was excited about my walk with Christ again. I was sure that I was on to something. The only problem was that it didn't last. Because I was dependent solely on my own strength to make the changes, I was soon back to rule-following and making sure that the outward "me" looked spiritual.

I put up a wall around other Christians for fear that they'd find out how unspiritual I was on the inside and think that I was a hypocrite. I desperately didn't want to be a hypocrite, but for all my effort and study I couldn't figure out how to fix the inside of me. I'd have victory for a while and then slip back into old ways of thinking.

I was convinced that a vibrant Christian life described in the Scriptures was real, but I just didn't know how to make it work. So I continued in an up-and-down, unsatisfying walk…sure of something more as the birthright of every believer but wholly unable to secure it for myself.

During this time, I was comfortable talking about God the Father and Jesus, but I avoided discussion of the Holy Spirit. I knew little about what the Holy Spirit was supposed to do in my life and had only a dry, textbook understanding of what it meant to be "filled with the Holy Spirit" or to "walk by the Spirit."

Then God most graciously gave me a visual aid in the lives of Pastor Robert Kuhns and his wife Astrida. Bob Kuhns came as an interim pastor to my church. From the first prayer meeting that they attended, one thing was clear – they knew how to genuinely love people. As the weeks went by, I watched them closely. They weren't perfect, but there was something different about the both of them. The fruit of the Spirit in their lives was the real deal – not the do-it-yourself, faked kind that Christians often substitute for the real thing.

On Memorial Day, Pastor Kuhns preached a message on how abundantly God forgives us. There was a noticeable joy in his voice. It was obvious that he really believed that what he was preaching was true and that he had personally experienced it. I'd never heard a pastor emphasize forgiveness like that; my mind had always interpreted the Scripture as saying, "Yes, God forgives, but only if you are really sorry for your sin and if you promise to never, never, ever do that sin again you vile little punk." My mind said that God grudgingly forgives because He has to – not because He wants to.

That sermon ignited something in my heart. I wanted to believe it was true. I wanted to replace my stern, judgmental God with a God who abundantly forgives, but I still wasn't sure that I could. For far too long I had functioned as a Christian believing that, even after confessing my sin, I had to mope around and kick myself for being such a rotten, inconsistent Christian. I told myself that I was a loser who could never be a good enough Christian to really please Jesus. I felt like a failure and a reject. I would have walked away from Christianity except that my whole life was wrapped up in Jesus. I didn't have anywhere else to go.

Several months later, Pastor Kuhns preached a message on the abundant life Jesus promised in John 10:10: *"The thief does not come except to steal, and to kill, and to destroy. I have come that they may have life, and that they may have it more abundantly."*

I wasn't able to be in that service, but I listened to the message online. Again, I heard that sheer joy in Pastor Kuhns' voice. What he was preaching clearly brought him great delight in his own personal life. It wasn't just theory; they had what I had been seeking for so many years, and it clearly worked for them. I sent them an email asking them to help me understand the abundant life. That began a two-year discipleship process during which God used them to dismantle the lies that I'd been believing – lies that kept me from the victorious Christian life.

Much of this book is about walking with the Holy Spirit and the process of replacing lies with the truth and believing facts rather than feelings. Any discussion of a satisfying Christian life needs to be squarely rooted in Scripture. Mystical, feelings-oriented approaches will not be effective or last. Any approach to godly living that puts *me* at the center will ultimately fail. A DIY foundation will always crumble.

Since making the change from do-it-yourself to walking by the Spirit, I've been tested by numerous trials and losses. But the abundant life has held. I no longer define God by what I see in the circumstances around me. Even when life isn't what I want it to be, I know with absolute certainty that God loves me and that He will always do what is right.

> *Even when life isn't what I want it to be, I know with absolute certainty that God loves me and that He will always do what is right.*

The life that Jesus designed for all His followers is that "something more" that you have been looking for. It's real. It's biblical. Come, let us follow the Shepherd and find the life which truly satisfies.

2

The Exquisite Gift of the Holy Spirit

"Then Peter said to them, 'Repent, and let every one of you be baptized in the name of Jesus Christ for the remission of sins; and you shall receive the gift of the Holy Spirit. For the promise is to you and to your children, and to all who are afar off, as many as the Lord our God will call'" (Acts 2:38-39).

Before Jesus ascended to Heaven after His resurrection, He told His disciples to wait for the Promise of the Father. That Promise was the gift of the Holy Spirit. He was given to the believers on the day of Pentecost.

We do not need to be afraid or uneasy with the concept of God the Holy Spirit – He is not spooky or mystical. He is defined in Scripture as the *Paraclete*, which translates into English as Comforter, Helper, Counselor, Advocate, or Friend.

The Holy Spirit is indispensable for all believers; He is the One who will transform them from vile sinners to redeemed saints. It is He that is primarily responsible for equipping the believer to live a holy and righteous life here on this side of heaven. This exquisite gift is everything we need for life and godliness. We do not need to be defeated by sin. By the power of the Holy Spirit, we can become like Christ our Savior. Amazing!

"For everyone who asks receives, and he who seeks finds, and to him who knocks it will be opened. If a son asks for bread from any father among you, will he give him a stone? Or if he asks for a fish, will he give him a serpent instead of a fish? Or if he asks for an egg, will he offer him a scorpion? If you then, being evil, know how to give good gifts to your children, how much more will your heavenly Father give the Holy Spirit to those who ask Him!" (Luke 11:10-13).

Beloved, the Holy Spirit is a really good gift. The best gift. But like a Stradivarius violin forgotten in a closet for 100 years, we may not know the treasure that we have.

There is much misinformation about who the Holy Spirit is and what He does, not because the Scriptures are silent on the matter but rather because people have either ignored the Scriptures or added their experiences to the Biblical record. Let's look at who the Holy Spirit is.

The Holy Spirit is fully God. As a Spirit, He has no physical body. However, He is not simply a power emanating from God. He is fully a Person. He can be fellowshipped with. He can be grieved, resisted, quenched, and blasphemed.

> *There is much misinformation about who the Holy Spirit is and what He does, not because the Scriptures are silent on the matter but rather because people have either ignored the Scriptures or added their experiences to the Biblical record.*

"But Peter said, 'Ananias, why has Satan filled your heart to lie to the Holy Spirit and keep back part of the price of the land for yourself? While it remained, was it not your own? And after it was sold, was it not in your own control? Why have you conceived this thing in your heart? You have not lied to men but to God'" (Acts 5:3-4).

Here Peter equates lying to the Holy Spirit with lying to God. The Holy Spirit is the third Person of the Trinity, having all the same abilities and attributes of God the Father and God the Son. As God the Father and

Jesus are all-knowing, all-powerful, everywhere present, sovereign, loving, gracious, faithful, merciful, and so on, so is the Holy Spirit. Because He is God, equal in essence to God the Father and Jesus Christ, He is worthy of worship. The Spirit will never act inconsistently from the Father and the Son.

The Holy Spirit is eternal – He has always existed and always will. He had a part in Creation with the Father and the Son. *"In the beginning God created the heavens and the earth. The earth was without form, and void; and darkness was on the face of the deep. And the Spirit of God was hovering over the face of the waters" (Genesis 1:1-2).* Job declares that *"by His Spirit He adorned the heavens."* The sun, moon, and billions of twinkling stars in the sky are all the handiwork of the Spirit. Some time ago, I was staying at a friend's house in rural South Dakota. I was outside a few hours before dawn while it was still quite dark. In the absence of manmade lights and obstructions on the horizon, I could see thousands of stars in the sky. It was breathtaking. The Holy Spirit designed that. He must love beauty.

The Holy Spirit is also the author of the Bible. *"And so we have the prophetic word confirmed, which you do well to heed as a light that shines in a dark place, until the day dawns and the morning star rises in your hearts; knowing this first, that no prophecy of Scripture is of any private interpretation, for prophecy never came by the will of man, but holy men of God spoke as they were moved by the Holy Spirit" (2 Peter 1:19-21).*

This will be significant when we begin to look at how the Holy Spirit guides and directs New Testament believers. The Spirit of God uses the very word of God that He authored. The Spirit does not supersede Scripture. His leading and guidance will always be in accord with what He has authored. He will not contradict Himself or His word.

But perhaps the most significant work of the Holy Spirit, from our perspective, is His essential work in the sanctification of each New Testament believer. The Holy Spirit is principally responsible in taking me from a stupid sinner to a satisfied, joyful saint.

The key to a confident, consistent spiritual life is yielding to and being controlled by the Holy Spirit. He is absolutely essential to every believer; one cannot effectively live the Christian life without the Holy Spirit. That is

> *The key to a confident, consistent spiritual life is yielding to and being controlled by the Holy Spirit.*

why every single believer is sealed and indwelt by the Holy Spirit from the moment of salvation.

"In Him you also trusted, after you heard the word of truth, the gospel of your salvation; in whom also, having believed, you were sealed with the Holy Spirit of promise, who is the guarantee of our inheritance until the redemption of the purchased possession, to the praise of His glory" (Ephesians 1:13-14).

The seal of the Holy Spirit attests to the fact that, at the moment of salvation, we are transferred from the kingdom of darkness into the kingdom of light. We went from being orphans to being the beloved children of our Heavenly Father. The seal is a declaration from God that He will never ever relinquish His grip on us.

"But you are not in the flesh but in the Spirit, if indeed the Spirit of God dwells in you. Now if anyone does not have the Spirit of Christ, he is not His. And if Christ is in you, the body is dead because of sin; but the Spirit is life because of righteousness. But if the Spirit of Him who raised Jesus from the dead dwells in you, He who raised Christ from the dead will also give life to your mortal bodies through His Spirit who dwells in you" (Romans 8:9-11).

There can be no such thing as a Christian without the Holy Spirit because the Bible declares, *"if anyone does not have the Spirit of Christ, he is not His."* The Holy Spirit is the seal of ownership.

In this book, we will discover much of what the Holy Spirit does in the lives of believers. It is not exhaustive – we will hit the highlights. We will see that it is the Holy Spirit who indwells believers and becomes their constant companion. He produces Christ-like character; He enables believers to have victory over sin. It is the Spirit who makes Christians fruitful in service, who reveals Jesus to believers and teaches them the Scriptures. He comforts, guides, strengthens, gives wisdom to, and intercedes for believers. When witnessing to the lost or giving testimony before persecutors, believers can depend on the Holy Spirit to give them the right words to say.

If you have ever felt like a failure in the Christian life, you owe it to yourself to discover all that the Holy Spirit wants to do on your behalf. Frustration and failure can be replaced by a transformed character and joy. You can be a legit disciple – both holy and free.

3

Be Filled with the Spirit

"And do not be drunk with wine, in which is dissipation; but be filled with the Spirit" (Ephesians 5:18).

The Bible commands us to "be filled with the Spirit." Nothing less is normative and acceptable in the life of a Christian.

In Galatians 5:16 we are told, *"I say then: Walk in the Spirit, and you shall not fulfill the lust of the flesh."* Several verses later, in Galatians 5:25, we read, *"If we live in the Spirit, let us also walk in the Spirit."*

How is a believer filled with the Holy Spirit? And what does "being filled with the Spirit" look like? How does a believer in practical, everyday terms walk by the Holy Spirit of God?

One Sunday morning service at my church, a family consisting of a father, mother, and a 20-something-year-old son sat in front of me. I was pretty sure that they were visitors because they looked a little unsure of themselves. While waiting for the service to start, I noticed that the grown son had a very short haircut. Then I noticed that a white scar dissected his head from the front to the back. During the early part of the service, a man from our church with terminal cancer spoke haltingly, thanking the congregation for the work they had done at his house the previous day – painting, cleaning, doing yard work, and cleaning his grill. He spoke confidently of his faith in God and His love. I noticed that the family sitting in front of me was listening intently. It was then that the Holy Spirit put the pieces together for me; the son was likely a patient at the Cleveland Clinic. Because of the proximity of our church to this world-renowned hospital, we often have visitors who are patients at the clinic.

After Hugh finished his testimony, my pastor desired to pray for him and his wife April. Pastor asked his own wife to come up front and stand by April. Then my pastor invited anyone else who needed prayer that morning to stand and challenged members of the congregation to come alongside them and put their hands on them as we prayed. I could see the son and his parents in front of me silently questioning one another about whether they should stand. They didn't.

The Holy Spirit had so convinced me of what was going on, though, that I felt perfectly confident to put one hand on the father's shoulder and one on the mother's as the congregation prayed. I knew that God had engineered the events of that morning because a family far from home was facing a scary and uncertain situation, and they needed to find hope and encouragement from Him. After the prayer, the wife turned around and said, "Bless you."

That morning, my pastor talked about a note he had received at a conference from another pastor. It was at a time when my pastor was going through a difficult period. The note card contained a verse that was particularly encouraging for his specific situation. For 12 years he has kept that card on his desk as a visible reminder of God's care for him at that time.

That morning I had put a small vial of mustard seed in my pocket. It had been a random, spur-of-the-moment decision as I was getting ready for church. But the Holy Spirit impressed on my heart that I needed to give that vial to the woman whose son was so ill so that she would have something to look at to remind her of His care. After the service, I learned that what I had discerned by the Holy Spirit was indeed correct. I handed her the vial of mustard seed, and she asked what it was. When I said "mustard seed," her eyes lit up and a smile covered her face.

God knew that morning that this family needed His touch and His assurance that He was right in the middle of their difficulty. This family had been directed to our church by the Spirit. The Spirit had guided my pastor and Hugh in what they said and did. And I too obeyed the promptings He was giving and went outside myself to do what He wanted done. I didn't second guess myself or fret about how I might come across. I simply obeyed. That family was blessed and I was blessed and God was glorified. And that is one example of what happens when believers are filled with the Spirit.

"And do not be drunk with wine...but be filled with the Spirit" (Ephesians 5:18).

Just as a person who is filled with wine is under the influence of the alcohol, so believers are to be under the complete influence of the Holy Spirit. We are to be controlled by the Holy Spirit and not to be under the control of other things. This is not a once-in-a-lifetime event; rather, it is an ongoing, moment-by-moment walking in unison with the Holy Spirit of God. The idea is that we would be so filled with the Spirit that there is no room for any other influence.

> *We are to be controlled by the Holy Spirit and not to be under the control of other things.*

A person who is drunk is "out of it," uninhibited and acting on impulse. Such people lack good reasoning and have slow reaction times. They draw attention to themselves by their out-of-control behavior. They are carried away by their own sin nature and the effect of the alcohol.

A person filled with the Spirit will be the exact opposite. People filled with the Holy Spirit of God will not be out of their minds or out of physical control of their bodies. They will not be acting out of a compulsion outside of themselves. Their focus will not be on bringing attention to themselves but rather toward making Christ known. As the Holy Spirit prompts them, they will speak truth rationally and with greater clarity. They will have increased discernment and humility. Their aim will be to give preeminence to Christ in all things. When the Spirit is active in a group, there will be a vertical, God-ward focus and also a noticeable unity among the members of the group. As they seek to draw near to God, they likewise draw near to each other.

In the spring of 2013, the Campus Bible Fellowship group at Cleveland State University was doing a fun event called an International Restaurant Hop. The idea was that we would enjoy appetizers at one international restaurant, the main course at a second, and then take desserts from an international bakery back to my apartment for a devotional time. There were 11 of us that night, when a Campus Bible Fellowship International missionary to Brazil shared her testimony. Trish's words resonated with the students in an unusual way. At the conclusion of her remarks, I suggested that we spend some time in prayer. The prayers were from the heart. One young woman, who had told me that she had been angry with God because of the difficulties in her life, completely broke down in repentance before God. A couple of guys in the group are sight-impaired, but their inability to see physical things has made them sensitive to spiritual things. They made their way over to the girl who was crying, put their hands on her shoulders, and began to pray for her. Another friend came over and also prayed a heartfelt prayer. I'm not sure how long we prayed, but it was prolonged and it was vertical.

We prayed until there wasn't anything more we felt we had to express. One of the guys pulled out his smart phone and began searching through his music list. At first I was taken aback by the abrupt change of activity, but he had a song that he thought would minister to the girl who was hurting. He found the song he was looking for and turned up the volume. The song spoke to each of us, and soon we were singing along, faces upturned to God, affirming to our heavenly Father that our hope was in Him to keep us steady and take us through the hard times. This was not a group of students who were normally expressive in their worship to God. There was no "worship leader" trying to generate some kind of feeling or experience – simply the Holy Spirit was leading and we were responding. We were drawn close to each other and close to our Savior. It was beautiful, peaceful, and calm.

Walking in the Spirit is synonymous with abiding in Christ. The two phrases are two ways to describe our union with Jesus Christ. Those that are filled with the Spirit are promised, *"Abide in Me, and I in you. As the branch cannot bear fruit of itself, unless it abides in the vine, neither can you, unless you abide in Me. I am the vine, you are the branches. He who abides in Me, and I in him, bears much fruit; for without Me you can do nothing...If you abide in Me, and My words abide in you, you will ask what you desire, and it shall be done for you. By this My Father is glorified, that you bear much fruit; so you will be My disciples" (John 15:4-5, 7-8).*

There are many things that would try to control us if we let them. Primarily, of course, is our sin nature or flesh. It will always rear its evil head looking for preeminence. Although the Spirit is constantly indwelling a believer, the filling of the Spirit and the resultant effect in the life of the believer is contingent on being in dependence on the Spirit and not grieving or quenching the Spirit through sin, rebellion, or self-sufficiency.

Addictions of any kind will inhibit the influence of the Holy Spirit; therefore, being a Spirit-filled believer will necessitate not being controlled by any other substance or compulsion. As Christians, we often think of addictions as being limited to drugs and alcohol. We think of the down-and-outer living on the sidewalk, not the person next to us in the pew.

However, there are a vast number of other addictions that exercise tremendous control over Christians. Fear, worry, unforgiveness, bitterness, hate, people-pleasing, discontent, perfectionism, and the pursuit of security and comfort often become driving forces in our lives and cause us to behave in ways inconsistent with faith in a holy God.

We can be controlled by our past or what other people think of us rather than by the Spirit of the living God. All these things that control us absolutely must be submitted to the Holy Spirit. The fruit of the flesh includes addiction. The fruit of the Holy Spirit includes self-control – the ability to regulate our thoughts, attitudes, and actions by the word of God.

Feelings of inferiority often fill an individual and usually control most aspects of his or her interactions with others. The world would tell us that people with low self-esteem or self-loathing need to learn to love themselves. But self-centered, narcissistic self-love is not the answer. Rather, the person plagued by self-loathing needs to open himself up to receive the love that God and others desire to extend to him.

In Christ we are supremely loved regardless of worth. No one *deserves* God's love. We are all broken, including those who look like they have it all together. Yet God Himself has purposed to love us based on who He is, not on who we are. His infinite grace extends to us because of the infinite love that defines who Christ is.

> *No one deserves God's love. We are all broken, including those who look like they have it all together. Yet God Himself has purposed to love us based on who He is, not on who we are.*

Our response can only be to accept that grace and be filled with the Spirit. We need to magnify Christ and allow His Spirit to flow through our lives. When we do that, we no longer need to hate what God has both created and claimed as His own. We need to become convinced that a loving Heavenly Father is looking out for us.

According to the Bible, people under the influence of God the Holy Spirit will be *"speaking to one another in psalms and hymns and spiritual songs, singing and making melody in your heart to the Lord, giving thanks always for all things to God the Father in the name of our Lord Jesus Christ, submitting to one another in the fear of God" (Ephesians 5:19-21).*

In other words, someone who is filled with the Spirit will be speaking about the Scriptures and spiritual songs; these people will be rejoicing in song; they will be thankful, and they will be submissive to one another.

Walking by the Spirit goes hand-in-hand with being filled by the Spirit. Walking by the Spirit is a day by day, hour by hour, moment by moment dependence and obedience to the indwelling Holy Spirit. It is the equivalent to being continuously filled with the Spirit.

The key is to orient our lives so that the Spirit can have full control. When I sense that I am operating in the flesh with a cranky, bad attitude, I can choose to turn, in dependence, to the Spirit and ask Him to fill me and retake control. (He loves to answer that kind of prayer.) We hinder the Holy Spirit's work in our lives when we grieve Him (Ephesians 4:30), resist Him (Acts 7:51) and quench Him (1 Thessalonians 5:19).

We grieve the Holy Spirit when we sin. The Spirit is holy, and sin in any form causes Him mental anguish. We know what it is to grieve a loss; we know the gut-wrenching sorrow of losing someone we love or the death of a dream. We are crushed; we feel physical pain and sometimes it hurts even to breathe. Grieving goes far beyond just being a little sad or annoyed. Sin is a serious thing. It necessitated Jesus Christ going to the cross. It causes deep sorrow in the Holy Spirit. Let us not belittle the impact of our sin.

Where there is disunity and disharmony among God's children, it causes the Holy Spirit to be grieved. In the Ephesians chapter four passage, Paul points to the destructiveness of lying, stealing, corrupt speech, bitterness, wrath, anger, malice, unforgiveness and broken relationships.

Jesus prayed in John 17:20-21: *"I do not pray for these alone, but also for those who will believe in Me through their word; that they all may be one, as*

You, Father, are in Me, and I in You; that they also may be one in Us, that the world may believe that You sent Me."

A hard heart grieves God, as does unbelief. God was grieved for 40 years with the Israelites in the wilderness because their hearts were hard and because they limited the Holy One of Israel by their unbelief in His power. Out of that unbelief, the Israelites rebelled against God's authority and disobeyed His command.

"But they rebelled and grieved His Holy Spirit; so He turned Himself against them as an enemy, and He fought against them" (Isaiah 63:10).

Resisting the Spirit is a form of rebellion. Suppose you are in a church service and the word of God is convicting your heart. There is an altar call and you know that the Spirit has spoken to you, but you refuse to go forward for fear of what people will say. You have resisted the Holy Spirit. Or, for example, you sense the Spirit leading you to give a large amount to a mission project but then decide that's too radical and you give $10 instead. You have resisted the Spirit. When the Spirit prompts your spirit to do something that is kind and does not contradict Scripture, it is wise to obey even if you are not 100% sure that prompting is of the Lord.

Of greatest consequence is to quench the Spirit. The word "quench" in the original Greek has the idea of "extinguishing" (Strong's Concordance). So to quench the Spirit is to extinguish the power and influence of the Holy Spirit in your life. When we quench the Holy Spirit, we have no more power over sin than an unbeliever has. When the Spirit is quenched, we operate exclusively in the sin nature until that time that we come to repentance. Believers who have quenched the Spirit have the capacity to do all manner of grievous sin and bring great dishonor to the name of God.

When I am grieving the Spirit, I will not be receiving His provisions for my well-being. His peace and comfort will be absent, as will His wisdom. Because I'm lacking His discernment, I'll make bad decisions. I will have anxiety. There will be a withdrawal of God's active grace and mercy in my life. My prayer life will dry up. I will have less and less appetite for the Bible. I will not be loving, joyful, peaceful, patient, good, kind, faithful, gentle, or self-controlled. I will be a messed up, miserable Christian.

So what quenches the Spirit of God? Pride quenches the Spirit, as does being unrepentant over sin, hiding or denying our sin, fearing man more than God, and ignoring the Spirit. Bitterness and a refusal to forgive someone who has wronged us also quenches the Spirit.

When we reject the Bible and do not read it, or when we refuse to obey its clear teachings, we hinder the work of the Holy Spirit in our life. The Spirit most often uses the Bible to do His work in and through our lives. To ignore Scripture and to depend on feelings or experiences that I attribute to the Spirit is to go down a path of self-deception. We must know Scripture in order to discern whether what we feel God telling us is really from Him.

If the impression that I am getting from God contradicts the teachings and principles of the Bible, my feeling is not from God, no matter how much my heart burns with it. It is always wise when trying to discern the Lord's leading in a decision to first ask the Lord to search your heart and see if there is anything that is grieving, resisting, or quenching the Spirit. Only a heart that is clear with the

> *If the impression that I am getting from God contradicts the teachings and principles of the Bible, my feeling is not from God, no matter how much my heart burns with it.*

Spirit will have the ability to discern properly. (We'll talk more about this in the chapter about the guidance of the Holy Spirit.)

Not every feeling or surge of emotion is the Holy Spirit. When the Spirit is at work, the result will be righteousness and truth. His fruit – love, joy, peace, patience, kindness, goodness, faithfulness, gentleness, and self-control – will be evident. Not everything that is mysterious or supernatural is from the Holy Spirit. Sometimes the source is only ourselves full of emotional energy. Satan also masquerades as an angel of light (2 Corinthians 11:14). He is a deceiver who, along with his demons, can counterfeit the works of God. During the ten plagues in Egypt, Pharaoh's magicians could replicate the first few plagues that God brought through the hands of Moses and Aaron.

We don't have the authority to declare that something is of the Holy Spirit if it does not have precedent in the Bible or if it is inconsistent with Scripture. We are not quenching the Spirit if we disallow some practices. For example, one of the fruits of the Spirit is self-control. Yet there are believers who would attribute all sorts of behavior where they lose control to the Holy Spirit. If a person is experiencing some manifestation where he is laughing inappropriately and uncontrollably, falling to the floor, or, in some other way, is unable to control himself, must we accept it as the work of the Spirit and assume that He has decided to countermand His own holy word? I don't think so. Paul, in 1 Corinthians 14:33, states that God is not the author of confusion. The Bible is full of declarations of what the Spirit does. When we look to see Him at work, we will see Him doing those things that He has promised to do.

"Beloved, do not believe every spirit, but test the spirits, whether they are of God; because many false prophets have gone out into the world. By this you know the Spirit of God: Every spirit that confesses that Jesus Christ has come in the flesh is of God, and every spirit that does not confess that Jesus Christ has come in the flesh is not of God. And this is the spirit of the Antichrist, which you have heard was coming, and is now already in the world" (1 John 4:1-3).

The opposite of quenching the Spirit is yielding to Him. *"Likewise you also, reckon yourselves to be dead indeed to sin, but alive to God in Christ Jesus our Lord. Therefore do not let sin reign in your mortal body, that you should obey it in its lusts. And do not present your members as instruments of unrighteousness to sin, but present yourselves to God as being alive from the dead, and your members as instruments of righteousness to God"* (Romans 6:11-13).

The antidote to grieving, resisting, and quenching the Spirit is to repent at the moment of conviction and receive Jesus' cleansing (1 John 1:9). Then, by the power of the Holy Spirit, resolutely obey whatever God has called you to do, asking Him to take control of you again. When sin is removed, the Spirit is set free to work in your life. By faith we can be consistently filled by the Holy Spirit and walk by the Spirit. We can go forth in confidence that He will take our frustrations and failures and turn them into triumphs of God's grace and glory.

4

Indwelt and Secure in the Holy Spirit

"And I will pray the Father, and He will give you another Helper, that He may abide with you forever"(John 14:16).

It is God who initiates a relationship with every believer and who does everything necessary at each step in the process to ensure that they will be with Him for all eternity. As the recipients of His love, we will ultimately be found and kept by our God. When we come to faith, we are given the Holy Spirit to help, guide, and keep us in this life and to see us successfully into eternity. He will live within us forever.

Before the foundation of the world, the Lord chose those who would believe according to the good pleasure of His will. *"Blessed be the God and Father of our Lord Jesus Christ, who has blessed us with every spiritual blessing in the heavenly places in Christ, just as He chose us in Him before the foundation of the world, that we should be holy and without blame before Him in love, having predestined us to adoption as sons by Jesus Christ to Himself, according to the good pleasure of His will, to the praise of the glory of His grace, by which He has made us accepted in the Beloved"* (Ephesians 1:3-6).

Of course, we weren't privy to that information when it happened. After we were physically born, however, God the Father began the process of wooing us to faith in Jesus Christ. *"For whom He foreknew, He also predestined to be conformed to the image of His Son, that He might be the firstborn among many brethren. Moreover whom He predestined, these He also called; whom He called, these He also justified; and whom He justified, these He also glorified. What then shall we say to these things? If God is for us, who can be against us? He who did not spare His own Son, but delivered Him up for us all, how shall He not with Him also freely give us all things?"* (Romans 8:29-32).

In this passage, all the actions of God – predestined, called, justified, and glorified – are in the past tense, revealing that in the mind of God they are already accomplished, even though glorification won't happen until we get to heaven. What God initiates, He commits Himself to complete.

"No one can come to Me unless the Father who sent Me draws him; and I will raise him up at the last day" (John 6:44).

"All that the Father gives Me will come to Me, and the one who comes to Me I will by no means cast out" (John 6:37).

"But as many as received Him, to them He gave the right to become children of God, to those who believe in His name: who were born, not of blood, nor of the will of the flesh, nor of the will of man, but of God" (John 1:12-13).

There came a day when I received Jesus Christ as my Savior. God the Father became my Father and I became His child. We entered into a covenant relationship, and the Father gave me the Holy Spirit both as a guarantee of His work for all eternity in my life and also as the Helper who would enable me to live a life that honors Jesus Christ. The Holy Spirit works within me to transform me from sinner to saint. All born-again believers are called "saints" – holy ones. It is the Holy Spirit who is actively working in each of us to make us pure and righteous like Christ.

"Now He who establishes us with you in Christ and has anointed us is God, who also has sealed us and given us the Spirit in our hearts as a guarantee" (2 Corinthians 1:21-22). The Holy Spirit of God is a promise that the work that God has begun in my life He will surely complete. At the moment of salvation, the Holy Spirit took up residence in my soul and became the seal that ensures that I will belong to Christ for all eternity.

"In Him you also trusted, after you heard the word of truth, the gospel of your salvation; in whom also, having believed, you were sealed with the Holy Spirit of promise, who is the guarantee of our inheritance until the redemption of the purchased possession, to the praise of His glory" (Ephesians 1:13-14).

God the Father, God the Son, and God the Holy Spirit work together to keep me secure. The person who is predestined in eternity past will be glorified in eternity future. Jesus affirms that He will raise that individual up at the last day.

Jesus promises: *"My sheep hear My voice, and I know them, and they follow Me. And I give them eternal life, and they shall never perish; neither shall anyone snatch them out of My hand. My Father, who has given them to Me, is greater than all; and no one is able to snatch them out of My Father's hand. I and My Father are one" (John 10:27-30).*

Years ago, when I was a missionary in Siberia, my coworkers' son was 3½ years old. We were crossing the street, and Deborah asked her son Sean to grab my hand to keep me safe as we crossed the road. Sean took his role of protector seriously. Obviously, however, the security of that street crossing was not dependent on one small boy. If he had decided to squirm and go his own way, I would not have let go of his hand. If he had tried to wiggle out of our grasp, I would have tightened my grip on his hand and exerted my authority. His safety was dependent on my being vigilant – even though he thought that responsibility was his. The Holy Spirit does the same thing with believers. At the first sign of our rebellion, the Holy Spirit gives a warning, then a tightening of the grip, and then chastening if necessary. The greater our rebelliousness is, the stronger the reaction of the Holy Spirit will be. But in no way will God simply let go of our hand and let us go play in traffic. He loves us too much for that.

Can a believer decide he or she no longer wants to believe and escape out of the hand of God? Can a mere man overrule the choosing, calling, and justifying work of God? Can we undo the seal of the Holy Spirit?

God the Father is greater than all. He will never relinquish what belongs to Him. You can squirm and you can fuss and you can make yourself miserable, but if you are truly born again, the Father is not letting go. Ever.

A person who rejects God after once walking with Him was probably not a true believer to begin with. *"They went out from us, but they were not of us; for if they had been of us, they would have continued with us; but they went out that they might be made manifest, that none of them were of us" (1 John 2:19).*

God let them go because they never belonged to Him in the first place. Many a person has had a form of religion without any power behind it. It is possible, of course, to grow up in the church and learn the lingo and what is expected behavior. Many have trusted in themselves and their righteousness rather than in the righteousness of Christ and the keeping of the Holy Spirit. At the Last Supper, when Jesus told His disciples that one of them would betray Him, there weren't 11 guys pointing at Judas. It wasn't obvious to the group who was unsaved among them. Likewise, someone can learn the Christian subculture and be considered a believer when he or she really is not.

Those that teach that believers can lose their salvation base that assumption on the holiness of God. They believe that because He is holy, He will not be mocked by out-of-control Christians who commit heinous sins. They assert that if believers think they can't lose their salvation, they will abuse that gift and sin willfully and without restraint. They believe that the fear of losing one's salvation is needed to keep believers in line and to control their behavior.

But does fear really motivate? Think of a groom saying to his beloved bride, "Honey, I love you. I love you more than life itself. I will give my life for you. However, if you ever commit adultery with another man, I will divorce you and you will go to hell. The Bible says that you must obey me and strive every day to live up to my standard. If you mess up too much, I won't put up with it and I will divorce you." Do you think that wife is going to have a happy marriage? Not likely. That woman will be fearful and insecure all the time. She will be constantly wondering if she has messed up too much.

On the other hand, a wife who is secure in the knowledge that her husband adores her is not going to be prone to sleeping with other men. Rather, she cherishes him and thrives under the knowledge of her husband's love and works diligently to please him in return.

The very ones who are the most likely to walk away from Christ are the ones who view Him as a distant, never-satisfied cosmic policeman.

The very ones who are the most likely to

walk away from Christ are the ones who view Him as a distant, never-satisfied cosmic policeman. Fear of God's wrath keeps them at a distance from God. The relationship is not a close one. And, therefore, they are not going to be dependent on the Holy Spirit to give them victory over sin. They will rely on their own efforts fueled by guilt and fear. Unfortunately, the flesh can never be depended on to do the right thing. As a result, many young people figure that they will never be good enough Christians to make it worth the effort and walk away from their faith rather than feel like a failure.

It is a dangerous practice to minimize God's love and abundant forgiveness in an attempt to keep errant believers in line. God Himself knows how to deal with His own rebellious children.

True believers who are secure in their relationship with God will sin less rather than more. Because the relationship is good and loving, they don't want to grieve the Spirit by deliberately sinning. They do not want to lose the blessings that God bestows on those who are walking obediently. *"Or do you not know that your body is the temple of the Holy Spirit who is in you, whom you have from God, and you are not your own? For you were bought at a price; therefore glorify God in your body and in your spirit, which are God's"* (1 Corinthians 6:19-20).

Eternal security does not mean lawlessness or license. Rather, it relies on the Holy Spirit to do His job of correcting and training and transforming the soul of each child of God. *"The LORD shall preserve you from all evil; he shall preserve your soul. The LORD shall preserve your going out and your coming in from this time forth, and even forevermore"* (Psalm 121:7-8).

When we sin, God the Father will bring chastening when necessary precisely because we are His children. He greatly desires our repentance and reconciliation.

"And you have forgotten the exhortation which speaks to you as to sons: 'My son, do not despise the chastening of the Lord, nor be discouraged when you are rebuked by Him; for whom the Lord loves He chastens, and scourges every son whom He receives.' If you endure chastening, God deals with you as with sons; for what son is there whom a father does not chasten? But if you are without chastening, of which all have become partakers, then you are illegitimate and not sons" (Hebrews 12:5-8).

According to this passage, if a believer can sin habitually and excessively with no consequences from God, then he did not lose his salvation. He never had salvation to begin with. Every son whom He receives, who is brought near to Him, is corrected when they are rebellious. Every single one. Only outsiders who don't belong to the family are not chastened when they sin. True believers will be corrected in love and for their profit. The purpose of God's chastisement is always reconciliation - not rescinding their going-to-heaven ticket.

"The Lord is not slack concerning His promise, as some count slackness, but is longsuffering toward us, not willing that any should perish but that all should come to repentance" (2 Peter 3:9).

Eternal security is dependent on the restorative power of repentance. *"If we confess our sins, He is faithful and just to forgive us our sins and to cleanse us from all unrighteousness...My little children, these things I write to you, so that you may not sin. And if anyone sins, we have an Advocate with the Father, Jesus Christ the righteous. And He Himself is the propitiation for our sins, and not for ours only but also for the whole world. Now by this we know that we know Him, if we keep His commandments. He who says, "I know Him," and does not keep His commandments, is a liar, and the truth is not in him. But whoever keeps His word, truly the love of God is perfected in him. By this we know that we are in Him" (I John 1:9; 2:1-5).*

> When we sin, Jesus is our Advocate, our defense attorney. He stands alongside us rather than turning His back in disgust. That doesn't mean that our sin isn't bad. It does mean that Jesus bears it for us.

When we sin, Jesus is our Advocate, our defense attorney. Jesus represents us to the Father. He stands alongside us rather than turning His back in disgust. That doesn't mean that our sin isn't bad. It does mean that Jesus bears it for us. He comes to help clean up the mess that our stubbornness and rebelliousness has created.

Can someone who once was a believer so grieve the Holy Spirit that it results in God casting him out? In the same sentence that the Bible warns about grieving the Holy Spirit, it reminds Christians that they were sealed for the day of redemption. *"And do not grieve the Holy Spirit of God, by whom you were sealed for the day of redemption" (Ephesians 4:30).* The implication is that because they are sealed for the day when they enter heaven, they should not grieve the One who holds them.

"For he who eats and drinks in an unworthy manner eats and drinks judgment to himself, not discerning the Lord's body. For this reason many are weak and sick among you, and many sleep. For if we would judge ourselves, we would not be judged. But when we are judged, we are chastened by the Lord, that we may not be condemned with the world" (1 Corinthians 11:29-32).

The implication here is that errant believers can be chastised severely – even onto death (*many sleep*) – but they don't lose their salvation. The name of Jesus is pure, and if we continue to bring shame on it, God may need to use such extreme measures. Salvation is not rescinded, but eternal rewards are lost.

John 3:16-17 promises everlasting life. *"For God so loved the world that He gave His only begotten Son, that whoever believes in Him should not perish but have everlasting life. For God did not send His Son into the world to condemn the world, but that the world through Him might be saved."* This fantastic promise means absolutely nothing if "everlasting" doesn't mean life that goes beyond my failures and my doubts. Everlasting life means never-ending life. It means life that doesn't quit.

When we are secure in our relationship with Jesus Christ, we can begin to appropriate all His marvelous promises that He has given us. *"Who shall separate us from the love of Christ? Shall tribulation, or distress, or persecution, or famine, or nakedness, or peril, or sword? As it is written: 'For Your sake we are killed all day long; we are accounted as sheep for the slaughter.' Yet in all these things we are more than conquerors through Him who loved us. For I am persuaded that neither death nor life, nor angels nor principalities nor powers, nor things present nor things to come, nor height nor depth, nor any other created thing, shall be able to separate us from the love of God which is in Christ Jesus our Lord"* (Romans 8:35-39).

We can have boldness and confidence in approaching Him. We need not be hindered by worry and fear. We will know that His grace is sufficient even in our darkest hours. *"But the Lord is faithful, who will establish you and guard you from the evil one"* (2 Thessalonians 3:3).

When we are assured of His Presence, we can face anything that this world throws at us because we know we are not alone. *"For He Himself has said, "I will never leave you nor forsake you"* (Hebrews 13:5b).

5

The Holy Spirit Transforms My Character

"But the fruit of the Spirit is love, joy, peace, longsuffering, kindness, goodness, faithfulness, gentleness, self-control. Against such there is no law" (Galatians 5:22-23).

The evidence of the Holy Spirit's work in my life will be a character that resembles Galatians 5:22-23. Our character – more than anything else – speaks of the influence of our Savior. For that reason, God is actively working to make us like Himself. He does not rely on our efforts to get the transformation done. If it was up to us to be holy, there would be nothing supernatural about it at all and God wouldn't get any of the credit.

Our character is the most effective sermon we will ever preach if we are filled by the Holy Spirit of God.

The greatest thing I have to glorify God is my character. If I do great

26

things but my character stinks, my good deeds will be marred. Our character is the most effective sermon we will ever preach if we are filled by the Holy Spirit of God.

"Now thanks be to God who always leads us in triumph in Christ, and through us diffuses the fragrance of His knowledge in every place. For we are to God the fragrance of Christ among those who are being saved and among those who are perishing. To the one we are the aroma of death leading to death, and to the other the aroma of life leading to life. And who is sufficient for these things?" (2 Corinthians 2:14-16).

"Not that we are sufficient of ourselves to think of anything as being from ourselves, but our sufficiency is from God, who also made us sufficient as ministers of the new covenant, not of the letter but of the Spirit; for the letter kills, but the Spirit gives life" (2 Corinthians 3:5-6).

When the Spirit is active in me, I will respond with kindness and patience when my buttons are pushed. I will be faithful to finish an unpleasant task. I will love the unlovable, even when the unlovable one is me. I will have joy in the midst of struggles. I will be humble instead of haughty. I will have control over what I say and what I do. It is not natural; it is supernatural. It is not the result of my own mastery over my emotions or will but rather the Spirit's mastery over my emotions and will. God wants to make us holy. He is up to the task. And no, dear friend, you are not too hard a case for Him.

Righteousness is not based on the law or our performance in living it out. Our righteousness is given to us by Jesus Christ because we need it – not because we deserve it or earned it.

When we came to faith in Christ, we gave Christ our sin and He in return gave us His righteousness. We gave Him our worst and He gave us His best. It is not our works that saved us, and it will not be our striving that makes us more like Christ. *"O foolish Galatians! Who has bewitched you that you should not obey the truth, before whose eyes Jesus Christ was clearly portrayed among you as crucified? This only I want to learn from you: Did you receive the Spirit by the works of the law, or by the hearing of faith? Are you so foolish? Having begun in the Spirit, are you now being made perfect by the flesh?" (Galatians 3:1-3).*

Our character is Christ's advertisement to the world. Therefore it is absolutely crucial that we are filled by the Holy Spirit of God. We must be diligent to remove all that would hinder that filling. As Christ flows through our lives, His Spirit produces fruit.

"For you were once darkness, but now you are light in the Lord. Walk as children of light (for the fruit of the Spirit is in all goodness, righteousness, and truth), finding out what is acceptable to the Lord" (Ephesians 5:8-10).

As you think back on your own spiritual growth, when were the times of greatest growth? When was there the most forward progress? It was probably the first few years after your conversion to Christ.

Young believers change rapidly as they are discipled; they are so in love with Jesus that they submit willingly to change. Often times their thinking changes, even without them intentionally wanting it to change. It just does. The Holy Spirit simply conforms them to the thinking of Christ.

The new believer may not even realize that his attitude has changed until something brings it to light. Before I received Jesus as my Savior when I was 24 years old, I was a liar. If the truth would make me look bad, I lied. Often I would make up elaborate stories to cover my tracks. But when Jesus came into my life, the Holy Spirit immediately began to address that defect in my character. But I didn't realize it until I found myself in a situation where I was asked to lie and I couldn't do it.

About a year after I was saved, I was working for a Girl Scout council in the Northwest. Our funding in part came from the United Way. Each year we had to submit a request to the United Way for funds. As an out-based field director for this council, my office was about two hours away from the main office. Late one Friday afternoon, I received the enrollment figures that my executive director had prepared for our presentation to the local United Way on that coming Monday. When I looked at the numbers, I was first confused, then shocked. The figures were considerably inflated.

I hoped it was just a mistake. I decided to call on Monday and clear up the confusion. So Monday morning I called my immediate supervisor and explained that I had received the wrong enrollment information. Brenda said she'd check with the executive director and call me back. A few minutes later she called and explained that the executive director had said that United Way funding was based solely on the number of people served in the previous year and so we needed to inflate the figures so that we would be granted enough funds to pay my salary. But I countered anxiously, "I'm a Christian and I can't lie. These figures are an outright lie."

Although sympathetic to my plight, Brenda reminded me that it was my salary that was on the line. "I can't lie," I said. A little over a year before, I had lied to my roommate because I'd borrowed her hammer and forgot to put it back. When she asked me if I had seen it, I bluntly said "no." Then I concocted an elaborate scheme so that she would "find" her hammer, rather than admitting the truth. But she didn't find the hammer, and after three days I had to "find" it for her. But now a lie was out of the question even if I lost my job. That was the effect of the Holy Spirit on my character.

We hung up and I called my pastor for prayer. His wife answered the phone and, after hearing my story, assured me that she and her husband would be praying. I calmed down and decided to go home for lunch. While at home, I began to analyze the enrollment numbers from the time I had arrived on the job a half year before. I was astounded. Since the arrival of a full-time staff member, the girl enrollment figures were way up. The true statistics were far better than the lies! When my executive director arrived at my office that afternoon, I was ready. Before she even had her coat off, I had both barrels blazing presenting my rationale for using the true half-year numbers instead of the fake full year ones. She told me that the members of the United Way committee already had the other figures. I told her that I couldn't lie. Finally she caved in and agreed to let me do the entire presentation. Praise the Lord.

The Holy Spirit coupled with His Word teaches the new believer what is wrong and what is right. Sins are removed, and good character is developed. In the first stage, the Holy Spirit is doing the work and we are just going along with it. The change is happening to us by the power of the Holy Spirit. He's in charge.

After that initial growth spurt, we should settle into a pattern of sustained growth to spiritual maturity. But sometimes this is where young believers get off track. Unless they have been instructed on the work of the Holy Spirit in sanctification, they may get the idea from sermons in church that they are the ones that need to get their act together. Often we get it into our heads that Christ did all the work to save us but now spiritual growth is our responsibility. We decide that we need to work hard to become more holy. We buy a lot of Jesus jewelry and a little fish symbol for our car bumper. We read the Bible, we attend seminars and take lots of notes, and we read Christian self-help books. But on the inside we don't change much. So we keep looking for *the* book or *the* program that will get us on track.

As we learn more, we tend to put the emphasis on knowledge. We think that if we know how we are to behave that we will be able to behave that way. We turn away from relying on the Spirit to change us and we focus on our own efforts to change. We berate ourselves when we fail and make more vows to do better. We heap on the guilt. We begin to conform ourselves to the Christians we hang out with rather than to Christ. Everything shifts to a human level.

We do "Christian nice" but make jokes about our lack of patience. We don't expect people to have joy or peace or genuine love. If they do have joy, we think they are faking it or that they don't live in the "real" world. We expect our fellow believers to have feet of clay and to struggle with godly character. So that no one feels too bad, we set the bar low and compare ourselves with ourselves and not with the example of Christ.

We focus on producing what I call "plastic fruit." In my own strength, I try to manufacture love, joy, peace, patience, kindness, goodness, faithfulness, gentleness, and self-control. It is largely a human effort based on a desire to please people and look spiritual to my peers. Somewhere along the line I have determined that I'm supposed to produce the fruit of the Spirit, but because my flesh is incapable of doing that I focus on externals.

> *Genuine spiritual fruit is the result of the Person of the Spirit — not the fruit of my best efforts.*

At a casual glance, plastic fruit might look real, but a closer look reveals it is fake. The only resemblance to the real thing is on the surface. One bite into a plastic apple is all it takes to realize that it is not going to satisfy. Inside, it is empty. Genuine spiritual fruit is the result of the Person of the Spirit — not the fruit of my best efforts.

The transformation of a Christian's character requires more than fleshly efforts. If we could clean ourselves up, Christ died on the cross in vain. Transformation requires the Holy Spirit's power and the believer's yielding to that power.

"Grace and peace be multiplied to you in the knowledge of God and of Jesus our Lord, as His divine power has given to us all things that pertain to life and godliness, through the knowledge of Him who called us by glory and virtue, by which have been given to us exceedingly great and precious promises, that through these you may be partakers of the divine nature, having escaped the corruption that is in the world through lust. But also for this very reason, giving all diligence, add to your faith virtue, to virtue knowledge, to knowledge self-control, to self-control perseverance, to perseverance godliness, to godliness

brotherly kindness, and to brotherly kindness love. For if these things are yours and abound, you will be neither barren nor unfruitful in the knowledge of our Lord Jesus Christ" (2 Peter 1:2-8).

Do you see the divine-human partnership in this passage? His divine power has given (past tense) all things needed for godliness through the knowledge of Him who called us by glory and virtue. He has given us what we require, but by faith we need to appropriate it by learning what He has provided. Then, God reminds us that He has given us (past tense) exceedingly great and precious promises that will enable us to partner with him and escape the corruption in the world. We are then exhorted to give all diligence to adding positive character traits into our lives. When I sense that my attitude is heading more to the flesh than the Spirit, I ask the Lord to fill me with His Spirit. Because God has so equipped us with everything we need for life and godliness, and because He has given us such exceedingly great and precious promises, we are to apply them with all expenditure of effort by faith in the Holy Spirit to enable us. By the enablement of the Holy Spirit, we put off evil characteristics and put on righteous ones.

The divine-human partnership is further illustrated in Matthew 11:28-30: *"Come to Me, all you who labor and are heavy laden, and I will give you rest. Take My yoke upon you and learn from Me, for I am gentle and lowly in heart, and you will find rest for your souls. For My yoke is easy and My burden is light."*

When we are in the yoke with Jesus we pull with all our might, but we are not wearied because Jesus is also pulling with His might. We do not carry the burden as much as He does, but we are not inactive.

If two animals connected by a yoke are not pulling at the same time, it is going to be painful for the slacker. The yoke will drag him along and chafe his neck. Spiritually, if we are not exerting effort to grow and are resistant to change, the yoke will chafe us. We will hinder the work that Jesus is attempting to do, and we will slow down our spiritual growth.

But when we gladly receive the yoke and eagerly endeavor to grow, fully confident that it is the Spirit working in us to produce the change, wonderful things will occur. We will mature and take on the character of Jesus Christ. The Christian who abides in Christ and allows the Spirit to make changes will more and more resemble his Master. These Christians will not be self-satisfied because they use Jesus Christ as their model and realize that they do not yet have His character fully molded in them.

"For what the law could not do in that it was weak through the flesh, God did by sending His own Son in the likeness of sinful flesh, on account of sin: He condemned sin in the flesh, that the righteous requirement of the law might be fulfilled in us who do not walk according to the flesh but according to the Spirit. For those who live according to the flesh set their minds on the things of the flesh, but those who live according to the Spirit, the things of the Spirit. For to be carnally minded is death, but to be spiritually minded is life and peace. Because the carnal mind is enmity against God; for it is not subject to the law of God, nor indeed can be. So then, those who are in the flesh cannot please God" (Romans 8:3-8).

What we could not do in the flesh, God did by sending His Son. He who calls us to be holy will make us holy as we yield to the Holy Spirit. Let us rest in that hope.

The Holy Spirit Gives Us
Victory Over Sin

"I say then: Walk in the Spirit, and you shall not fulfill the lust of the flesh"
(Galatians 5:16).

As Christians, we desire to be holy. We desire to live up to what the Bible says that we ought to be. We desire to please the Lord. But if we are honest with ourselves, we fail. We fail a lot.

"For I know that in me (that is, in my flesh) nothing good dwells; for to will is present with me, but how to perform what is good I do not find. For the good that I will to do, I do not do; but the evil I will not to do, that I practice. Now if I do what I will not to do, it is no longer I who do it, but sin that dwells in me. I find then a law, that evil is present with me, the one who wills to do good. For I delight in the law of God according to the inward man. But I see another law in my members, warring against the law of my mind, and bringing me into captivity to the law of sin which is in my members. O wretched man that I am! Who will deliver me from this body of death?" (Romans 7:18-24).

Too often our Christian walk is a "body of death" – a never-ending cycle of temptation, sin, broken fellowship with God, repentance and reconciliation, temptation, sin, broken fellowship with God, repentance. We have little victory over sin and even less joy.

Many religions teach that man has to be good and that those good deeds, if there are enough of them to outweigh the bad in his life, will give him a place in heaven. Salvation becomes the result of self-effort. But the Bible is different. It affirms that man's best deeds – his finest moments – are filthy rags.

"But we are all like an unclean thing, and all our righteousnesses are like filthy rags; we all fade as a leaf, and our iniquities, like the wind, have taken us away" (Isaiah 64:6).

The old nature (i.e. the flesh) is corrupt, and there is no hope for cleaning it up. It will remain corrupt all our days. *"That you put off, concerning your former conduct, the old man which grows corrupt according to the deceitful lusts..."(Ephesians 4:22).* But when we received Jesus Christ as Savior, we were changed forever. We were given a new, righteous nature. *"...and that you put on the new man which was created according to God, in true righteousness and holiness" (Ephesians 4:24).*

In addition, the Holy Spirit came to indwell us from the moment of salvation.

"Therefore, from now on, we regard no one according to the flesh. Even though we have known Christ according to the flesh, yet now we know Him thus no longer. Therefore, if anyone is in Christ, he is a new creation; old things have passed away; behold, all things have become new" (2 Corinthians 5:16-17).

Obviously we can (and still do) sin. At any given moment in our day, we can live in the flesh (sin nature) or live in the Spirit (new nature). There is no middle ground. We are either controlled by the Spirit or controlled by the flesh moment by moment. Either self is in charge or the Spirit is. And it can change instantly.

But now sin has become an unnatural act for us. Our identity has changed. When we fail, we do not cease to belong to Him, and we do not cease to be saints. We are saints who sin, doing an act which is contrary to our new nature that we received from Christ.

Satan would have us think that we are fundamentally unchanged – that we are still sinners bound by sin. But that is a deception. It is a lie, but unfortunately a lie that binds many a saint. Many saints spend their whole lives trying to measure up to God's standards and feeling like failures before

God and hypocrites before men. They don't believe that they have what it takes to be righteous.

Satan, the accuser, tries to convince us that, when we sin, we are alienated from God and that God is unwilling to forgive. He tells us that we are losers unworthy of God's love. He tells us that our relationship with our Savior is dependent on how well we measure up to God's standards. Often Christians agree with Satan and conclude that they are losers. They heap guilt on themselves in hopes that they will shape up and quit doing all the sinful, rotten, vile things that they do. They punish themselves with condemning thoughts.

Too often Christians try to be holy by their own strength – trying to do all the right things so that God will be pleased. It sounds pious. The Scriptures say, "Be holy for I am holy." But they use the wrong tools. They rely on the do–it–yourself approach – self-discipline and rules they devise for themselves and guilt to make themselves behave properly. In response to failure they redouble their efforts with more willpower, more self-discipline, more guilt, more penance, more vows to change. But using more of the wrong tool doesn't make it the right tool.

In a pinch, sometimes a wrench can be used as a hammer. You might succeed in getting the nail into the wall. But it doesn't make sense to ignore the hammer in favor of a wrench for hammering nails. In the same way, relying on your own self-discipline to combat sin may work on occasion, but it isn't a long-term solution.

God's provision for our holiness is the Holy Spirit of God. He is meant to be the primary agent in our sanctification. He is the One that enables us to have victory over sin and to exhibit true Christian character. Remove God the Holy Spirit from our

God's provision for our holiness is the Holy Spirit of God. He is the One that enables us to have victory over sin and to exhibit true Christian character. Remove God the Holy Spirit from our theology and we are Pharisees trying to obey the law by the power of the flesh.

theology and we are Pharisees trying to obey the law by the power of the flesh. The entire Old Testament teaches us that in our flesh we are incapable of living holy lives.

"Therefore by the deeds of the law no flesh will be justified in His sight, for by the law is the knowledge of sin" (Romans 3:20).

The law shows us God's standard and our inability to keep it by our good intentions and effort. *"Knowing that a man is not justified by the works of the law but by faith in Jesus Christ, even we have believed in Christ Jesus, that we might be justified by faith in Christ and not by the works of the law; for by the works of the law no flesh shall be justified. But if, while we seek to be justified by Christ, we ourselves also are found sinners, is Christ therefore a minister of sin? Certainly not! For if I build again those things which I destroyed, I make myself a transgressor. For I through the law died to the law that I might live to God. I have been crucified with Christ; it is no longer I who live, but Christ lives in me; and the life which I now live in the flesh I live by faith in the Son of God, who loved me and gave Himself for me. I do not set aside the grace of God; for if righteousness comes through the law, then Christ died in vain" (Galatians 2:16-21).*

Perhaps we make attachments to the wrench to make it more like a hammer, and it works a little better. In the Christian realm, when we find that our own self-discipline isn't the answer to our sin problem, we look to others to govern over us and hold us accountable.

We resort to fear of man and his penalties to keep us in line. And that often works to control the exterior. But it does little to change the heart and creates a prime soil for the weeds of duplicity, hypocrisy, judgmentalism, legalism, and lack of integrity to grow.

We focus on the externals. Outward conformity dupes us into thinking we aren't that bad. We judge our righteousness not by Christ but by the people around us. We manage our sin on the outside and put on a happy mask when we go to church. When people ask how we are, we use the obligatory answer: "Fine." We put up a wall around ourselves for fear other Christians will find out how unspiritual we are on the inside. The inner man and the outer man do not match. We don't want to be hypocrites, but no matter how hard we try, we can't seem to figure out how to fix the inside.

Fear of man shifts the focus from a change of heart to a pursuit of not getting found out. We feel like a hopeless loser among a church full of people with their acts together. But the truth is, all of us, if we are doing the Christian walk as a do-it-yourself project, have the walls out of plumb.

God has designed a better way – a far better way. *"I say then: Walk in the Spirit, and you shall not fulfill the lust of the flesh. For the flesh lusts against the Spirit, and the Spirit against the flesh; and these are contrary to one another, so that you do not do the things that you wish. But if you are led by the Spirit, you are not under the law"* (Galatians 5:16-18).

The Holy Spirit is the primary provision that God has given us for victory over sin. Beloved, by faith we need to appropriate the tool God has given us.

The word "walk" is an English translation of a Greek word *peripateo*, which means "to walk around, live, conduct oneself or to be a devoted and faithful follower of a leader or ideal" (Strong's Concordance). We are to be faithful followers of the Holy Spirit.

When I was a kid, we used to play "Follow the Leader." The game was simple. All you had to do was follow behind the leader and copy each thing that the leader did. If the leader waved his hand, so did you. If the leader skipped, so did you. The moment that you started doing your own thing, however, was the moment that you were out of the game. That's how we are to walk by the Spirit. We are to follow His lead and do what He does. We are to obey His leadership.

But how do you follow a leader that you cannot see? Yep, that's the problem. Because we can't see the Holy Spirit, we need to develop our other senses in order to follow Him well. *"For we walk by faith, not by sight"* (2 Corinthians 5:7). The more we know the Word that He has written, the more that the Spirit can use it to direct us. He can warn us of approaching sin by bringing a verse or a biblical concept to mind. When we get a check in our Spirit (that uneasy feeling in our gut that what we are about to do is unwise), we need to stop and reevaluate our actions and ask the Lord to fill us with the Spirit and get us back on track. Those little promptings are the voice of the Spirit, but our spiritual hearing can get desensitized if we don't pay attention. If we are constantly overriding the voice of the Spirit, we will no longer be sensitive to His promptings. We are grieving the Spirit. But the more we respond to those little nudges, the more accurate we get in hearing the voice of the Spirit. Obedience is key to spiritual growth.

In my own journey, the more I accepted God's love, grace, and forgiveness and became secure in His love for me, the more godly I became. Because the relationship was close and I could trust Him, I did not want to offend Him or quench or grieve the Holy Spirit. My own guilt trips never gave me victory over sin. Freedom does. Let God work on your sin nature.

He is perfectly capable of producing Christ-likeness in you. The Apostle Peter's second letter affirms that *"the Lord knows how to deliver the godly out of temptations and to reserve the unjust under punishment for the day of judgment" (2:9)*.

It is helpful to understand how the Holy Spirit works to give us victory over sin. When we recognize what He is doing, we are better able to respond and yield our will to His.

Step 1 – Warning and a way of escape

"No temptation has overtaken you except such as is common to man; but God is faithful, who will not allow you to be tempted beyond what you are able, but with the temptation will also make the way of escape, that you may be able to bear it. Therefore, my beloved, flee from idolatry" (1 Corinthians 10:13-14).

Every one of us will face temptation multiple times in a day. If we are walking by the Spirit, we will sense the Spirit's warning when faced with temptation. We will sense that we are in a precarious position or that the thing we are beginning to contemplate is wrong. If we are obedient to the Holy Spirit, we will take the way of escape and stop moving toward that sin. Most often, the way of escape is getting out of the place that we are in. When faced with temptation, we need to stop, pray, and turn away. Praying without turning away doesn't usually help much. But trying to turn away without the Holy Spirit's help usually doesn't happen either. Fighting the flesh with the flesh isn't very successful.

> *As long as we define that sin as "good," we will be tempted and operating in the flesh. When we try to justify something that we know to be wrong, we deceive ourselves.*

It is not enough to tell ourselves "this is wrong" but continue to think about the sin that attracts us. The pull of sin will only get stronger and our willpower will only get weaker. Therefore, we need to respond decisively and ruthlessly by the power of the Holy Spirit. To have victory over sin, we must deliberately redirect our thinking and move from operating in the flesh to operating in the Spirit. As long as we define that sin as "good," we will be tempted and operating in the flesh. When we try to justify something that we know to be wrong, we deceive ourselves. But when we see it as God sees it, we will realize that it is not good. If something is sin, by definition it is harmful.

"For the weapons of our warfare are not carnal but mighty in God for pulling down strongholds, casting down arguments and every high thing that exalts itself against the knowledge of God, bringing every thought into captivity to the obedience of Christ" (2 Corinthians 10:4-5).

We need to remind ourselves that the temptation is not omnipotent. It can be resisted with the help of the omnipotent Holy Spirit. The goal is to be obedient to the Holy Spirit's prompting. Instead of responding in anger towards the person who just insulted us, we will take a deep breath, pray for the Spirit's control, and deliberately respond in kindness. We must switch off the racy show on TV or turn off the computer instead of feeding our sexual interest. When we are walking by the Spirit, we will stop being alone with our boyfriend in his dorm room late at night. We will admit the intense power of sin and our inability to combat it in the flesh. We won't pridefully think we can handle it. We'll get serious about holiness and not try to manage our sin habit.

"Blessed is the man who endures temptation; for when he has been approved, he will receive the crown of life which the Lord has promised to those who love Him. Let no one say when he is tempted, 'I am tempted by God'; for God cannot be tempted by evil, nor does He Himself tempt anyone. But each one is tempted when he is drawn away by his own desires and enticed. Then, when desire has conceived, it gives birth to sin; and sin, when it is full-grown, brings forth death. Do not be deceived, my beloved brethren" (James 1:12-16).

Step 2 – Confession and getting back on track

Despite our best intentions, however, there will be times when we override the Holy Spirit's warning and plunge headlong into sin. It takes only seconds to respond in anger to an unkind remark or to envy a coworker who got the promotion. It's easy to get drawn into complaining with our friends. As the Holy Spirit convicts us of our sin, we realize that we have just committed the very same sin that has plagued us over and over. We know we are guilty. We feel like losers. We wonder if we will ever mature in our Christian walk.

When we fail, are we destined to be out of fellowship with God for a time until we can work our way back into His good graces? No! We can immediately be restored as soon as the Spirit convicts us of sin. In the heat of the moment we can stop, confess our sin, and receive the Lord's forgiveness and cleansing.

God has a solution for your sin. It's called repentance. At the moment that you realize you have sinned, you will find God ready and willing with the remedy.

"If we confess our sins, He is faithful and just to forgive us our sins and to cleanse us from all unrighteousness. If we say that we have not sinned, we make Him a liar, and His word is not in us. My little children, these things I write to you, so that you may not sin. And if anyone sins, we have an Advocate with the Father, Jesus Christ the righteous. And He Himself is the propitiation for our sins, and not for ours only but also for the whole world. Now by this we know that we know Him, if we keep His commandments. He who says, 'I know Him,' and does not keep His commandments, is a liar, and the truth is not in him. But whoever keeps His word, truly the love of God is perfected in him. By this we know that we are in Him" (I John 1:9-2:5).

Beloved, when God cleanses us, He cleanses us completely. My sins and yours are gone. We were decimated by sin, but Jesus has paid the price for our iniquities. We are free! Believe it. Thank Him. Praise Him. Love Him. Live for Him.

We must not wallow in our own failure, heaping on the guilt. Rather, we must stand resolutely on the truth of Scripture rather than our own feelings. When we confess our sins, He cleanses us from all unrighteousness. And, rather than being distant and ticked off at us for our sin, Jesus becomes our Advocate before the Father. When we are stinking guilty and admit it to God, Jesus comes alongside us to be our Advocate. Instead of being a stern and angry judge, He is our defense attorney.

> *When we truly understand the depth of love that makes a holy God put up with us, we should forever banish the thought of happily indulging in sin figuring that we will simply confess it later and God will forgive.*

When we truly understand the depth of love that makes a holy God put up with us, we should forever banish the thought of happily indulging in sin figuring that we will simply confess it later and God will forgive. Only a jerk happily grieves the very ones who love him most and takes advantage of their kindness and forgiveness.

"Keep back Your servant also from presumptuous sins; let them not have dominion over me. Then I shall be blameless, and I shall be innocent of great transgression. Let the words of my mouth and the meditation of my heart be acceptable in Your sight, O LORD, my strength and my Redeemer" (Psalm 19:13-14).

When we walk by the Spirit, we will look at sin as God looks at sin – as so vile that it cost Jesus His blood. To have victory over sin, we must remember that God the Father, Jesus, and the Holy Spirit are grieved by our sin. They are not unaware or indifferent to our acts of rebellion. The One who loved us so much that He did everything to reconcile us with Himself is sorrowed when we sin.

My relationship with God is what is important. I choose not to sin because I want that relationship to be close. *"If you love Me, keep My commandments. And I will pray the Father, and He will give you another Helper, that He may abide with you forever—the Spirit of truth, whom the world cannot receive, because it neither sees Him nor knows Him; but you know Him, for He dwells with you and will be in you. I will not leave you orphans; I will come to you"* (John 14:15-18).

Step 3 – Chastening

Sometimes we don't walk by the Spirit because we have a stubborn streak in our nature. It's not that we don't think that the Spirit is right. It's not that we don't understand that what we are about to do is wrong. We are just stubborn and want to control our own destinies. We want the little adrenaline rush of doing something that is dangerous or forbidden.

We want freedom. But freedom from God's active grace and mercy and presence in our lives is the greatest source of bondage there ever was! We are in bondage to our own pride and stupidity.

"Woe to those who call evil good, and good evil; who put darkness for light, and light for darkness; who put bitter for sweet, and sweet for bitter! Woe to those who are wise in their own eyes, and prudent in their own sight!" (Isaiah 5:20-21).

Sin is so appealing and our rebellion is so strong that all thoughts of yielding to the Spirit get squashed if we are not diligent to have an attitude of submission. As we head down the path of gratifying our sinful natures, the question is not so much "can't" as "won't." It's not that my tongue is unable to tell the truth but that it won't.

If we ignore the Holy Spirit, we will be incapable of living a victorious Christian life. If we persist in sin, the cost of that sin will increase. Our pain will increase. Our lives will get complicated. Why? Because our Holy Father loves us too much to let us go our own way.

"And you have forgotten the exhortation which speaks to you as to sons: 'My son, do not despise the chastening of the Lord, nor be discouraged when you are rebuked by Him; for whom the Lord loves He chastens, and scourges every son whom He receives.' If you endure chastening, God deals with you as with sons; for what son is there whom a father does not chasten? But if you are without chastening, of which all have become partakers, then you are illegitimate and not sons. Furthermore, we have had human fathers who corrected us, and we paid them respect. Shall we not much more readily be in subjection to the Father of spirits and live? For they indeed for a few days chastened us as seemed best to them, but He for our profit, that we may be partakers of His holiness. Now no chastening seems to be joyful for the present, but painful; nevertheless, afterward it yields the peaceable fruit of righteousness to those who have been trained by it" (Hebrews 12:5-11).

When God chastens His child, He does it "in love" and "for our profit." God is not on a power trip. He's a Father concerned about the choices His kid is making, knowing that heartache is in store for His beloved child if He doesn't intervene.

By the time we need chastening, we have already grieved and resisted the Holy Spirit. We aren't listening, so God will need to use pain of some sort to get our attention. Oftentimes corrective pain comes about as the natural consequence of our sin. God doesn't have to bring difficulty; we've already invited difficulty to dinner. Our self-centeredness has caused our relationships to get out of whack. Our choices have gotten us in trouble with the authorities in our lives.

Because the Spirit is grieved or quenched, we do not receive the necessary provisions that God has given us. There is a quenching of the power and felt presence of the Spirit. God seems distant. We will lack peace and comfort. There may be a withholding of God's grace in our lives. As I ignore fellowship with God, I end up being pretty much on my own with only my own resources to get through life. And that's going to bring a lot of ouch.

"Behold, the LORD'S hand is not shortened, that it cannot save; nor His ear heavy, that it cannot hear. But your iniquities have separated you from your God; and your sins have hidden His face from you, so that He will not hear" (Isaiah 59:1-2).

The purpose of God's chastening is to bring us to repentance and confession of our sin. He is eager to see us repent so that He can lavish His forgiveness on us. The relationship will be restored immediately and completely as soon as we turn to Him. He will not put us on probation. Rather the floodgates of His grace will be opened and we will be thoroughly cleansed and restored.

"And you, being dead in your trespasses and the uncircumcision of your flesh, He has made alive together with Him, having forgiven you all trespasses, having wiped out the handwriting of requirements that was against us, which was contrary to us. And He has taken it out of the way, having nailed it to the cross" (Colossians 2:13-14).

When chastening comes our way, we need to submit to it. We need to ask the Lord to reveal whatever sin is in our life, and when He does, we need to repent of it. We need to quit justifying our sin and humble ourselves before God. Because we know that confession brings unhindered fellowship with Christ, we are wise to open up our whole lives to Christ. When we do, we will be received by Him and have all that is Christ's at our disposal.

The Holy Spirit is Our Comforter

"And I will pray the Father, and He will give you another Helper, that He may abide with you forever--the Spirit of truth, whom the world cannot receive, because it neither sees Him nor knows Him; but you know Him, for He dwells with you and will be in you. I will not leave you orphans; I will come to you" (John 14:16-18).

This passage is one of Jesus' last instructions to His disciples before He went to the cross. He was soon to be leaving them physically, and He wanted them to know they weren't being abandoned.

"But the Helper, the Holy Spirit, whom the Father will send in My name, He will teach you all things, and bring to your remembrance all things that I said to you. Peace I leave with you, My peace I give to you; not as the world gives do I give to you. Let not your heart be troubled, neither let it be afraid" (John 14:26-27).

The Holy Spirit is called the Helper, Comforter, and Counselor depending on the translation of the Bible that you prefer. The Holy Spirit is all of these. He will always be there to help, comfort, console, intercede, and advocate when we truly need it. He will give us courage and sustain us.

The word in the original Greek is *Parakletos*, which is defined as "intercessor" or "consoler" (Strong's Concordance). An intercessor makes an appeal on behalf of another. A consoler seeks to relieve the sorrow or grief of someone else. Comfort means "to soothe in time of affliction or distress; to ease physically."

Notice in all of these definitions that the one who is comforted is in trouble, grieving, or suffering. The Holy Spirit comforts, but it is not His purpose to make us comfortable. He soothes in times of affliction and distress, but doesn't coddle in times of ease.

Here in the United States we have embraced comfort as an inalienable right. That is not the goal of the Holy Spirit. He desires to give us strength and courage to go on — not a robe and fuzzy slippers and an easy chair. Pain-free cannot be the goal of life. We live in a fallen world. Bad stuff happens. We have to go through difficult things that we desperately don't want to go through. But as Spirit-filled Christians, we can have emotional stability in the midst of trial and glorify God in the process.

> *Often when we are hurting, we look everywhere for comfort except to the Holy Spirit.*

Often when we are hurting, we look everywhere for comfort except to the Holy Spirit. We look to people who will tell us what we want to hear; others turn to alcohol or drugs or a bag of Oreos. We escape into movies, our music, video games, and virtual environments. But those sources of comfort are temporary at best. To be victorious in the midst of suffering, believers must depend on the Source of all comfort.

"Blessed be the God and Father of our Lord Jesus Christ, the Father of mercies and God of all comfort, who comforts us in all our tribulation, that we may be able to comfort those who are in any trouble, with the comfort with which we ourselves are comforted by God. For as the sufferings of Christ abound in us, so our consolation also abounds through Christ" (2 Corinthians 1:3-5).

We will only find lasting comfort from the Holy Spirit. Because He is infinite and perfect, He understands you better than you understand yourself. He weeps when you weep. *"You number my wanderings; put my tears into Your bottle; are they not in Your book? When I cry out to You, then my enemies will turn back; this I know, because God is for me. In God (I will praise His word), in the LORD (I will praise His word), in God I have put my trust; I will not be afraid. What can man do to me?" (Psalm 56:8-11).*

How does the Holy Spirit provide comfort for the sons and daughters of God? First of all, He comforts through the promise of His Presence. The verse at the beginning of this chapter promises that He will "abide with you forever" and that He "dwells with you and will be in you." Nothing is going to come into your life that He doesn't notice.

"Let your conduct be without covetousness; be content with such things as you have. For He Himself has said, 'I will never leave you nor forsake you.' So we may boldly say: 'The Lord is my helper; I will not fear. What can man do to me?'" (Hebrews 13:5-6).

"Fear not, for I am with you; be not dismayed, for I am your God. I will strengthen you, yes, I will help you, I will uphold you with My righteous right hand" (Isaiah 41:10).

Live by faith, confident that He is continually with you, bringing all His resources to bear on your difficulty. He knows. He cares.

"Therefore humble yourselves under the mighty hand of God, that He may exalt you in due time, casting all your care upon Him, for He cares for you" (1 Peter 5:6-7).

A second way that the Holy Spirit brings comfort is through the Bible, which He authored. His word is a comfort. It teaches us what God is like and what He has promised His children. The accounts of how He dealt with believers who have gone before us give us courage because we know that we serve the same God.

"For whatever things were written before were written for our learning, that we through the patience and comfort of the Scriptures might have hope. Now may the God of patience and comfort grant you to be like-minded toward one another, according to Christ Jesus, that you may with one mind and one mouth glorify the God and Father of our Lord Jesus Christ" (Romans 15:4-6).

The Bible reminds us of what is true and unchanging when our thoughts are skewed by our feelings and circumstances. A lot in this world can tear us down. The Bible reminds us how much we are loved by an infinite God and how abundantly our holy Heavenly Father forgives when we confess our sin. It shows us that God stands ready to reconcile us to Himself.

"Remember the word to Your servant, upon which You have caused me to hope. This is my comfort in my affliction, for Your word has given me life" (Psalm 119:49-50).

Another way the Holy Spirit comforts believers is by His peace. We do not live in a peaceful world. Even if our own surroundings are relatively calm, the internet and television showcase the chaos from around the world. Hardly a day goes by without some gruesome tragedy happening somewhere in our world. If we pay attention to it all, we can put ourselves on a constant state of alert. Yet Jesus declares: *"These things I have spoken to you, that in Me you may have peace. In the world you will have tribulation; but be of good cheer, I have overcome the world"* (John 16:33). What a wonderful promise. Nothing is going to happen in our lives that hasn't first gone through the hands of the Lord Jesus Christ. We are not helpless victims.

"You will keep him in perfect peace, whose mind is stayed on You, because he trusts in You. Trust in the LORD forever, for in Yah, the LORD, is everlasting strength" (Isaiah 26:3-4).

When I was a missionary in the Far East of Russia, there was a point near the end of my ministry in the town of Vanino when, due to a change in the laws, our religious workers' visas could not be renewed. My coworkers were forced to depart and were harassed and questioned extensively on their way out of the country. I stayed behind to take care of the church building and the congregation of mostly women and children. I was pretty sure that I was being watched by immigration authorities. The combination church and parsonage building was surrounded by a tall chain-link fence. Each night after dark I went out to the gate and secured it with a padlock and chain. I was under the impression that the chain link fence and the locked gate would protect me from anyone who desired to do me harm.

Late one night after I had chained the gate, I heard a persistent knock at the front door. Two men stood there asking to speak to the "Padre." I refused to let them in, as I was the only one there. Eventually (after several minutes of pleading), they left the way they had come – by walking over the chain-link fence. The snow that spring in late March was still so deep that walking over the fence was really not that difficult for a moderately tall individual. Later I surmised that the men were probably connected to the church on Sakhalin Island and had hoped to spend the night free of charge at our church, but nevertheless my confidence in the fence was shattered.

The next night I had to go to sleep knowing that my only protection was the Lord Jesus Himself.

The Baptist Mid-Missions home office had promised to pray each morning for me. Their prayer time in Cleveland, OH coincided with my bedtime in the Russian Far East. As I lay there and prayed, an amazing thing happened. I became overwhelmingly sleepy and a peace enveloped me. Within minutes I dropped into a deep, worry-free sleep and slept soundly until morning.

"Peace I leave with you, My peace I give to you; not as the world gives do I give to you. Let not your heart be troubled, neither let it be afraid" (John 14:27).

The faithfulness of God is also a means of His comfort. *"Even to your old age, I am He, and even to gray hairs I will carry you! I have made, and I will bear; even I will carry, and will deliver you"* (Isaiah 46:4).

God, by the power of the Holy Spirit, carries us. *"But we have this treasure in earthen vessels, that the excellence of the power may be of God and not of us. We are hard pressed on every side, yet not crushed; we are perplexed, but not in despair; persecuted, but not forsaken; struck down, but not destroyed...Therefore we do not lose heart. Even though our outward man is perishing, yet the inward man is being renewed day by day. For our light affliction, which is but for a moment, is working for us a far more exceeding and eternal weight of glory, while we do not look at the things which are seen, but at the things which are not seen. For the things which are seen are temporary, but the things which are not seen are eternal"* (2 Corinthians 4:7-9, 16-18).

The Lord is not disengaged or distant or holding out on you. He is lovingly there and trying to carry you. But you must submit to it. We allow ourselves to be carried when we humbly acknowledge our hurt and our need to our Father. We need to go to God as our comforter rather than as our enemy. We must cry out for help rather than accuse Him of neglect or of mismanaging our lives. In our pain we must draw near to God rather than cutting off all communication. The Holy

> *The Lord is not disengaged or distant or holding out on you. He is lovingly there and trying to carry you. But you must submit to it.*

Spirit will have more difficulty convincing you of His comfort if you aren't in communication with Him.

Remember God's attributes. He is stronger than people and overrules the wicked plans of men. Don't let your feelings overpower what the Scriptures clearly say about God. Your feelings and perceptions are impacted by pain and are not a reliable indicator of truth at the moment. Hold tight to God's goodness, care, and infinite power, even when you have more questions than answers. The Holy Spirit is near to those with a broken heart.

After acknowledging our hurt, we must permit the Holy Spirit to take us through the grieving process. It takes time, but the Holy Spirit is a professional comforter. He knows how to lead us through the darkness to a place of contentment and light. We can trust Him to take us through the process. Then when we begin to recognize the new opportunities that God is opening up, we start looking forward rather than just looking back at our loss. We acknowledge that God still has good things for us in the future.

"The steps of a good man are ordered by the LORD, and He delights in his way. Though he fall, he shall not be utterly cast down; for the LORD upholds him with His hand" (Psalm 37:23-24).

8

The Holy Spirit Teaches Us the Scripture

"I still have many things to say to you, but you cannot bear them now. However, when He, the Spirit of truth, has come, He will guide you into all truth; for He will not speak on His own authority, but whatever He hears He will speak; and He will tell you things to come. He will glorify Me, for He will take of what is Mine and declare it to you. All things that the Father has are Mine. Therefore I said that He will take of Mine and declare it to you" (John 16:12-15).

When Jesus was in the upper room with His disciples before His death, He had many things to say to them. He desired to instruct them in the things of God so that they would understand what was about to happen. He wanted to establish them in their faith and prepare them for when He would no longer be on earth. He wanted to equip them to take the message of salvation to the Jews and then to the entire world. But there was a limit to what they could take in.

Later, after His death and resurrection, they were still confused and shaken. They did not understand what His death had accomplished. Three and a half years of walking with Jesus and hearing His teaching had not been enough. So Jesus gave them divine help. *"And He opened their understanding, that they might comprehend the Scriptures" (Luke 24:45).*

Jesus' teaching would continue through the Holy Spirit, but not just to the eleven disciples. Every believer would be taught His Word via the indwelling Spirit of God.

"But you have an anointing from the Holy One, and you know all things...But the anointing which you have received from Him abides in you, and you do not need that anyone teach you; but as the same anointing teaches you concerning all things, and is true, and is not a lie, and just as it has taught you, you will abide in Him" (1 John 2:20, 27).

Through the anointing of the Holy Spirit given to every believer, we will be able to learn and grow to spiritual maturity. The deep and wonderful truths of the word of God are not just for professional theologians. The Holy Spirit seeks to use the Word of God in the lives of every believer to help them grow up in Christ.

The gift of the Holy Spirit is given so that we may be complete in Christ. He is to be our personal instructor who not only knows His subject intimately but also authored the textbook. Of course, as in all things related to spiritual growth, this process of being taught by the Spirit is a divine-human partnership. We must develop the anointing – this endowment of the Spirit – by studying and pondering the truths of God, praying, and asking for more insight. The Holy Spirit is eager to instruct any who desire to learn and apply the Word of God. The Holy Spirit dwelling within us is "the mind of Christ" which 1 Corinthians 2:16 declares we possess. We can walk in truth because we have Truth indwelling us.

That is not to say that we shouldn't take opportunities to learn from others who are walking with Christ. The Holy Spirit uses pastors, teachers, and other believers to teach, give understanding, and develop spiritual maturity. *"And He Himself gave some to be apostles, some prophets, some evangelists, and some pastors and teachers, for the equipping of the saints for the work of ministry, for the edifying of the body of Christ, till we all come to the unity of the faith and of the knowledge of the Son of God, to a perfect man, to the measure of the stature of the fullness of Christ; that we should no longer be children, tossed to and fro and carried about with every wind of doctrine, by the trickery of men, in the cunning craftiness of deceitful plotting" (Ephesians 4:11-14).*

God has given us human teachers that He has equipped. The best teachers will be the ones who challenge you to go back to the Bible to see if what they are saying is true. Paul applauded the believers in Berea because *"these were more fair-minded than those in Thessalonica, in that they received the word with all readiness, and searched the Scriptures daily to find out whether these things were so"(Acts 17:11).*

> *Do not let the difficult passages in the Bible deter you from studying the Word in reliance upon the Holy Spirit.*

Do not let the difficult passages in the Bible deter you from studying the Word in reliance upon the Holy Spirit. Commit to obeying by the enablement of the Holy Spirit that which is clear and you will grow tremendously in your faith. Over time, many of the perplexing passages will become comprehensible.

"Teach me, O LORD, the way of Your statutes, and I shall keep it to the end. Give me understanding, and I shall keep Your law; indeed, I shall observe it with my whole heart. Make me walk in the path of Your commandments, for I delight in it. Incline my heart to Your testimonies, and not to covetousness. Turn away my eyes from looking at worthless things, and revive me in Your way. Establish Your word to Your servant, who is devoted to fearing You" (Psalm 119:33-38).

It takes time and effort and waiting upon the Lord to understand the more complex truths of the Bible. It's easier to be spoon-fed on Sundays and take someone else's word for what the Bible says. Don't give in to that temptation.

"For though by this time you ought to be teachers, you need someone to teach you again the first principles of the oracles of God; and you have come to need milk and not solid food. For everyone who partakes only of milk is unskilled in the word of righteousness, for he is a babe. But solid food belongs to those who are of full age, that is, those who by reason of use have their senses exercised to discern both good and evil" (Hebrews 5:12-14).

We should never quit learning; we should not plateau and become self-satisfied in our spiritual knowledge. *"For this reason we also, since the day we heard it, do not cease to pray for you, and to ask that you may be filled with the knowledge of His will in all wisdom and spiritual understanding; that you may have a walk worthy of the Lord, fully pleasing Him, being fruitful in every good work and increasing in the knowledge of God; strengthened with all might, according to His glorious power, for all patience and longsuffering with joy; giving thanks to the Father who has qualified us to be partakers of the inheritance of the saints in the light" (Colossians 1:9-12).*

What tremendous things could be accomplished for the Kingdom of God if every believer was actively studying the Scriptures under the illumination of the Holy Spirit! God has so much He would desire to do through us if we would determine to move on from spiritual babyhood and mature in our understanding of His Word.

The Holy Spirit Testifies of Jesus

"But when the Helper comes, whom I shall send to you from the Father, the Spirit of truth who proceeds from the Father, He will testify of Me. And you also will bear witness, because you have been with Me from the beginning" (John 15:26-27).

For those of us who missed seeing Jesus Christ in the flesh by about 2,000 years, the Holy Spirit plays a vital role in understanding who Jesus is and what He is like. Christianity is so much more than a set of wise sayings and teachings. At its heart, it is a commitment to a Person.

Although we have not physically walked with Jesus, we can still come to know Him. As the indwelling Holy Spirit speaks of Jesus through the Scriptures, our God becomes less of a nebulous ideal and more of a concrete Person in our minds. That's a very good thing.

"However, when He, the Spirit of truth, has come, He will guide you into all truth; for He will not speak on His own authority, but whatever He hears He will speak; and He will tell you things to come. He will glorify Me, for He will take of what is Mine and declare it to you. All things that the Father has

are Mine. Therefore I said that He will take of Mine and declare it to you"
(John 16:13-15).

The Holy Spirit does not speak from His own authority. The Trinity is always a unity. The Spirit glorifies Jesus by speaking what He has been given to speak. Jesus, also, did not speak His own words but brought glory to the Father. *"If anyone wants to do His will, he shall know concerning the doctrine, whether it is from God or whether I speak on My own authority. He who speaks from himself seeks his own glory; but He who seeks the glory of the One who sent Him is true, and no unrighteousness is in Him"* (John 7:17-18). The fact that the Holy Spirit glorifies the Son rather than Himself should not be construed to mean that the Holy Spirit is a lesser partner in the Trinity. All are God, and thus all are worthy of our worship and attention.

Without the Holy Spirit witnessing of Jesus, we might be prone to define Jesus the way we wish Him to be rather than who He is. Oftentimes people with a specific agenda make statements about what Jesus would do or not do based more on their own agenda than a careful analysis of the life of Jesus. These assessments of Jesus are often one-dimensional.

Jesus was never a one-dimensional person. As a relatively young man, at the age of thirty He began His ministry. He chose twelve other young men to be His disciples – a handful of Galilean fishermen, a tax collector who made money by collaborating with Rome, and a revolutionary who desired to see Rome overthrown. He completely bypassed the religious professionals in forming His group of twelve disciples. He did what was right rather than what the establishment expected. He seemed to delight in provoking the Pharisees by healing on the Sabbath. He could be kind to those who realized their sinfulness and angry with the self-righteous who condemned others. He treated women with bad reputations with respect. He talked about loving your neighbor as yourself and turning the other cheek when you were struck.

If Jesus' church acted more like Jesus, the church

If Jesus' church acted more like Jesus, the church would probably have fewer enemies for the wrong reasons and more for the right ones.

would probably have fewer enemies for the wrong reasons and more for the right ones. People would reject Christianity because of Jesus and His teachings rather than because of the behavior of His disciples who aren't imitating His example.

"He who says he abides in Him ought himself also to walk just as He walked" (1 John 2:6). Through the Holy Spirit operating in our minds and hearts we can by faith walk as Jesus walked and testify of Him to a world that needs to know Him.

In the 1990s there was a fad among evangelical Christians of wearing bracelets, necklaces, and T-shirts inscribed with the letters W.W.J.D. The acronym stood for "What Would Jesus Do?" The modern day disciples of Jesus were challenged to live like the One that they said they followed. But it was obvious that a lot of people wore the jewelry but never studied the Bible to genuinely answer the question.

We cannot accurately answer "What Would Jesus Do?" if we don't have the Holy Spirit to reveal Jesus to us through the Scriptures. Although we can read the Bible for ourselves, we often need the Holy Spirit to make the connections. The Holy Spirit helps the Scriptures to come alive and helps us to put ourselves into the story and imagine what it was like to walk with Jesus. On our own it is too easy to make Bible reading mechanical – reading words without the implications soaking into our thinking.

I remember a while back when I spent some time thinking about what it would have been like to be among the crowds as Jesus was healing people. Sunday school pictures depict everyone calmly standing around in a quiet, orderly gathering. But was that what it was like? If a person who had been lame for years could suddenly walk, would he calmly shake Jesus' hand, say thank you, and stroll back to his home? Or would he be jumping and shouting and high-fiving everyone around him? Would people be politely waiting their turn or pushing and shoving to get to the front of the line? My guess is that those healing sessions were not quiet, orderly events.

Did Jesus get tense at all the demands or was He patient and kind? Of course, when the Scripture is silent we ought not to write in details. But many times the details are there if we pay attention with the assistance of the Holy Spirit. As you read, invite the Spirit to reveal the Scriptures to you.

Years ago, during a time of illness between ministry assignments, I spent about two months studying the attributes of God. I spent a week on each character trait – searching for each occurrence in the Scriptures and then prayerfully summarizing in my own words what the Bible was saying. On all eight of the attributes that I studied, the Holy Spirit brought clarity and conviction. I had to confess that although I spoke all the right truths, I wasn't actually living in complete confidence of their authenticity. Knowing Jesus better intellectually then led to knowing Him better experientially. *"And those who know Your name will put their trust in You; for You, LORD, have not forsaken those who seek You"* (Psalm 9:10).

As believers in God, we are to put on the character of Jesus Christ. As the only Person of the Trinity to have taken on a human body and experienced human situations, Jesus Christ becomes our example of what it looks like to be godly in human form. *"That the God of our Lord Jesus Christ, the Father of glory, may give to you the spirit of wisdom and revelation in the knowledge of Him, the eyes of your understanding being enlightened; that you may know what is the hope of His calling, what are the riches of the glory of His inheritance in the saints, and what is the exceeding greatness of His power toward us who believe, according to the working of His mighty power"* (Ephesians 1:17-19).

Because He is infinite and we are finite, we will never know everything there is to know about the Lord. We can continue all our days to delight in knowing Him better and better. *"One thing I have desired of the LORD, that will I seek: that I may dwell in the house of the LORD all the days of my life, to behold the beauty of the LORD, and to inquire in His temple"* (Psalm 27:4).

> *As the only Person of the Trinity to have taken on a human body and experienced human situations, Jesus Christ becomes our example of what it looks like to be godly in human form.*

10

The Holy Spirit Equips Us for Service

"Now concerning spiritual gifts, brethren, I do not want you to be ignorant...There are diversities of gifts, but the same Spirit. There are differences of ministries, but the same Lord. And there are diversities of activities, but it is the same God who works all in all. But the manifestation of the Spirit is given to each one for the profit of all" (1 Corinthians 12:1, 4-7).

The Holy Spirit gives each believer one or more spiritual gifts in order to equip him or her to serve the Lord Jesus Christ. No one is exempt. Since all Christians are to be servants, all are given at least one spiritual gift to use in ministering to others.

"As each one has received a gift, minister it to one another, as good stewards of the manifold grace of God. If anyone speaks, let him speak as the oracles of God. If anyone ministers, let him do it as with the ability which God supplies, that in all things God may be glorified through Jesus Christ, to whom belong the glory and the dominion forever and ever. Amen" (1 Peter 4:10-11).

A spiritual gift is a God-infused ability given to a believer by the Holy Spirit for the building up of Christ's church. 1 Corinthians speaks of spiritual gifts "for the profit of all." Ephesians chapter 4 says that the gifts are for "the edifying of the body of Christ." Although we will enjoy using our gift, it is not given to us for our own profit. Spiritual gifts are given to us to make us useful. No one gift is superior to the others. All are valuable to the health of the body of Christ.

Theologians differ on how many gifts there are and even on the definition of the various gifts that are mentioned. Many books have been written that seek to define what the Bible leaves undefined. In fact, movements and denominations have formed because of differing views of certain gifts. We will not add to that discussion here.

Partial lists of spiritual gifts are found in Romans 12:3-8, 1 Corinthians 12:7-11, 28, and Ephesians 4:11-12.

"For I say, through the grace given to me, to everyone who is among you, not to think of himself more highly than he ought to think, but to think soberly, as God has dealt to each one a measure of faith. For as we have many members in one body, but all the members do not have the same function, so we, being many, are one body in Christ, and individually members of one another. Having then gifts differing according to the grace that is given to us, let us use them: if prophecy, let us prophesy in proportion to our faith; or ministry, let us use it in our ministering; he who teaches, in teaching; he who exhorts, in exhortation; he who gives, with liberality; he who leads, with diligence; he who shows mercy, with cheerfulness" (Romans 12:3-8).

"But the manifestation of the Spirit is given to each one for the profit of all: for to one is given the word of wisdom through the Spirit, to another the word of knowledge through the same Spirit, to another faith by the same Spirit, to another gifts of healings by the same Spirit, to another the working of miracles, to another prophecy, to another discerning of spirits, to another different kinds of tongues, to another the interpretation of tongues. But one and the same Spirit works all these things, distributing to each one individually as He wills…And God has appointed these in the church: first apostles, second prophets, third teachers, after that miracles, then gifts of healings, helps, administrations, varieties of tongues" (1 Corinthians 12:7-11, 28).

"And He Himself gave some to be apostles, some prophets, some evangelists, and some pastors and teachers, for the equipping of the saints for the work of ministry, for the edifying of the body of Christ" (Ephesians 4:11-12).

Gifts are for the building up of the Lord's church. Some of the gifts were vital for the establishment of the early church to authenticate the message (and the messenger) prior to the completion of the New Testament. Paul defended his apostleship to the church in Corinth: *"I have become a fool in boasting; you have compelled me. For I ought to have been commended by you; for in nothing was I behind the most eminent apostles, though I am nothing. Truly the signs of an apostle were accomplished among you with all perseverance, in signs and wonders and mighty deeds"* (2 Corinthians 12:11-12).

Because the Bible is now complete, we have the means to validate whether a speaker is from God or not based on whether his or her teaching lines up with the written word. Therefore, the authenticating or "sign gifts" are no longer necessary.

"But whether there are prophecies, they will fail; whether there are tongues, they will cease; whether there is knowledge, it will vanish away. For we know in part and we prophesy in part. But when that which is perfect has come, then that which is in part will be done away" (1 Corinthians 13:8b-10).

Other spiritual gifts such as pastor/teacher, administration, mercy, service, evangelism, giving, and exhortation are for the building up and sustaining of Christ's church. Therefore, these and other similar gifts will continue to be given in the life of the church until Christ returns.

> *The Holy Spirit has set each person in the body of Christ in the way that He chooses. He gives us gifts that fit with the personality He has given us.*

The Holy Spirit has set each person in the body of Christ in the way that He chooses. Each follower of Jesus has a function, and each should be serving. Because God created us with a specific goal in mind, He gives us gifts that fit with the personality He has given us. God doesn't work at cross purposes with Himself. *"For we are His workmanship, created in Christ Jesus for good works, which God prepared beforehand that we should walk in them"* (Ephesians 2:10).

What an amazing thought! God has already designed works for me to do. It follows, then, that He is also designing me for those works. The personality and interests that He has put in me are there for a purpose. I don't have to become an entirely different person in order to serve God. What a relief!

So how do I determine my gift (or gifts)? Start by serving the Lord. Experiment with different areas of service. See what you like to do and what you are good at. What gives you joy? Pray. Ask other mature Christians who have seen you serve what they perceive as your gifting.

We are to be dependent on the Holy Spirit to define our gifts and to guide us in the development and use of them. As we develop our gift, we will enjoy it. Other people will be blessed. There will be spiritual fruit.

Your gift is who you are designed to be in the church. If you are not serving in your local church, then your church has a hole and something that God considers important is being neglected or perhaps is being done by someone who is not gifted for that particular need. The church is designed to be a living, interdependent organism.

"For as the body is one and has many members, but all the members of that one body, being many, are one body, so also is Christ. For by one Spirit we were all baptized into one body--whether Jews or Greeks, whether slaves or free-and have all been made to drink into one Spirit. For in fact the body is not one member but many. If the foot should say, 'Because I am not a hand, I am not of the body,' is it therefore not of the body? And if the ear should say, 'Because I am not an eye, I am not of the body,' is it therefore not of the body? If the whole body were an eye, where would be the hearing? If the whole were hearing, where would be the smelling? But now God has set the members, each one of them, in the body just as He pleased. And if they were all one member, where would the body be? But now indeed there are many members, yet one body. And the eye cannot say to the hand, 'I have no need of you'; nor again the head to the feet, 'I have no need of you.' No, much rather, those members of the body which seem to be weaker are necessary. And those members of the body which we think to be less honorable, on these we bestow greater honor; and our unpresentable parts have greater modesty, but our presentable parts have no need. But God composed the body, having given greater honor to that part which lacks it, that there should be no schism in the body, but that the members should have the same care for one another. And if one member suffers, all the members suffer with it; or if one member is honored, all the members rejoice with it" (1 Corinthians 12:12-26).

I remember one summer when I dislocated and broke my pinkie finger on my right hand. I thought, "It's a small, insignificant part. This will not be a big deal." And yet my entire routine was impacted by that small, insignificant part. I had trouble dressing myself, tying my shoes, spreading peanut butter on a piece of toast, and driving a car. There was very little that I could do smoothly and efficiently. The same is true with a church where not all the members are utilizing their gifts and serving. It is not good when a believer with the gift of exhortation is teaching the toddler Sunday school class. Likewise, someone with the gift of mercy or service might be a poor fit for door-to-door evangelism.

It's clear that for a healthy church or fellowship group we need each other. But sometimes the gifting can be a source of tension between believers because they forget that the ability that they have is a supernatural thing given to them by God because of grace. We cannot boast about what we have received as a gift as though it was our own superiority that merited it.

I remember when I was a young missionary in Russia; there was a lady in our church who would give testimony during the services of her evangelistic efforts. She would glowingly report how she had come across a drunken man and exhorted him to turn to Christ. She shared Scripture with him until he fell to his knees weeping and confessing Christ as Savior. From the way she gave her testimony, it was clear that she thought all of us should be out there leading drunks to Christ. Since it was easy for her, she assumed that it should be easy for everybody. In her manner she insinuated that the rest of us were slackers because we didn't do what she did.

I felt inferior and deficient in my zeal for the Lord. As an unbeliever, I hated being the recipient of such evangelistic efforts and would turn away from seeking Christ when strangers forcefully assaulted me with the "if you were to die tonight" line. Even after I was saved, I empathized with the guy on the street too much to feel good about going up to strangers and giving them a canned presentation concerning their eternal destiny. But because this woman presented street evangelism as THE way to serve Jesus, I felt that I must be lacking in love for Christ. At the time, it didn't dawn on me that I didn't have the gift of evangelism, and that is why I couldn't do (and didn't want to do) what this woman did.

Your spiritual gift is your role in the local church. It comes easy to you and the temptation is to think that anyone can do it because it is "easy." But it is not easy for someone who is gifted in a different way. One couple I know is especially gifted in the areas of service and giving. They are very practical, anticipating the needs of others. They can pull off a dinner for 50 people without much trouble. They anticipate people's financial needs and quietly go about meeting those needs. They share freely what they have and apologize for not being able to do more. But because their gift is so easy for them, they don't think that what they do is anything special. They assume that anyone could do what they do. But not anyone can. Rather than saying their ministry is not important, it might be better to acknowledge God's work in their lives by saying, "This is how God has gifted us. All the glory goes to Him." That frees others from feeling deficient for not being able to be such tremendous hosts.

It is important that we do not compare ourselves with other believers. God does not compare His children and ask why we are not like so-and-so. He *knows* why we are not like so-and-so. Because HE hasn't given us the spiritual gifts that He has given to that other person. He has designed us for something else.

We ought to delight in others when they utilize their spiritual gift – without making comparisons to our own lack of that particular gift. When we have this attitude, the whole church is blessed. We must acknowledge that what they are so good at is a *spiritual* gift and not just a natural talent. And we need to acknowledge that the Holy Spirit knows what He is doing in our case. There is no need to be jealous or feel inferior or compare one with another. We just need to delight ourselves in discovering and developing our own gifts from the Holy Spirit.

> *We ought to delight in others when they utilize their spiritual gift – without making comparisons to our own lack of that particular gift. When we have this attitude, the whole church is blessed.*

There are times, however, as we walk with the Spirit, that God uses us to do some service for Him that is outside our usual gifts. The Holy Spirit infuses a situation with power. As we minister filled with the Holy Spirit, our inadequacies melt away and He simply takes over, giving us moment-by-moment wisdom and guidance. He will provide the necessary tools for the ministry. He will remove the roadblocks. He also works in the hearts of those that receive our ministry, bringing them to a place of receptivity. Here the Holy Spirit may enable believers to do something well that they are not gifted for or He will enhance the gift and make it even more effective.

The Campus Bible Fellowship group at Cleveland State University decided that they wanted to do an outreach event on campus the week before Easter. It was thrilling to watch as the Holy Spirit put together that event. One day the two students who were in charge of the event and I met to find a suitable location on campus and to decide on a theme for the worship event. We went to Conference Services and found that they had three rooms that would be the size that we thought we would need available on the day that we wanted to do the event. So we went to go look at the rooms. The first two were locked, and neither was suitable for what we wanted to do. The third room was unlocked. We went inside and found it to be just what we wanted. We decided to sit down there and pray, committing the event to the Lord and asking for His wisdom regarding a theme. Our prayers acknowledged our desire for God's plans rather than our own. As we prayed, we sensed we were on holy ground.

After spending some time in prayer, we began discussing possible themes. After some time we had decided on a particular theme. Although I didn't have a sense of the Spirit's confirmation, the other women seemed to like it. A bit later I saw that one of the ladies was sort of disengaged from the conversation. I knew she was hungry because she had told us so before the meeting. I assumed that she was thinking about dinner. However, the question that came out of my mouth was, "What ya thinking?" She answered something like, "I'm just thinking of how marvelous God's forgiveness is and how much He has forgiven me; even when I was being rebellious and trying to do my own thing and doing stuff I knew I shouldn't be doing, He came after me and dragged me out of there."

We all began thinking along those lines and we realized that God's Spirit had just revealed our theme – "Forgiven." There was just a worshipful, vertical spirit among us. We knew we were in the presence of the Lord.

In the weeks leading up to the Forgiven Easter worship service, the Lord continued to lead us step by step. Much prayer was devoted to the event. The Holy Spirit worked marvelously in the CBF students who were part of the service. Each one did his or her part beautifully.

The service was particularly worshipful and vertically God-focused. The students were so filled with love for their Lord that it didn't seem as though they were in any way self-conscious. Normally shy and reserved students seemed to have no nervousness, hesitation, or fear. Each portion of the service flowed into the next. Even Scripture readings were so powerful that people applauded after the verses were read. The student who preached his first sermon that night handled the word of God with skill.

At the end, I gave an invitation appealing to people to ask Jesus to search their hearts and to show them any sin that needed His forgiveness or whether they needed to come to Him for salvation. I encouraged them to write whatever their sin was on slips of paper that we had on the tables and then to bring those papers to a wooden cross that we had in the front of the room with the words from Colossians 2:13-14 on the upright beam. They were to take their paper, cover it with a tag with the word "FORGIVEN" written on it in red, and then nail it to the cross with a pushpin.

As soon as the prayer concluded, people were grabbing pens and paper. Soon there was a line at the cross.

Sometimes we get hung up on our own inadequacies. We think that we do not have much to offer God and, therefore, that we are not important to His work. Nothing could be further from the truth.

Nearly every person in the room responded in some way. The Holy Spirit led that event from the fledging idea to do "something" at Easter to what He continues to do in the hearts of those who were there. No human could get the praise for that event.

Sometimes we get hung up on our own inadequacies. We think that we do not have much to offer God and, therefore, that we are not important to His work. Nothing could be further from the truth. Our limitations are not important to God in regards to His ability to use us. On the other hand, neither is He impressed by or dependent on our strengths. God doesn't need to call capable, talented people to get His work done. Sometimes those are the last people He calls because they tend to work in their own strength and He needs people dependent on His Holy Spirit to get the job done.

"Not that we are sufficient of ourselves to think of anything as being from ourselves, but our sufficiency is from God, who also made us sufficient as

ministers of the new covenant, not of the letter but of the Spirit; for the letter kills, but the Spirit gives life" (2 Corinthian 3:5-6).

The Holy Spirit is Our Guide

"However, when He, the Spirit of truth, has come, He will guide you into all truth; for He will not speak on His own authority, but whatever He hears He will speak; and He will tell you things to come" (John 16:13).

The guidance that the Holy Spirit gives us starts by teaching us the Scriptures so that we may know how we ought to live. *"All Scripture is given by inspiration of God, and is profitable for doctrine, for reproof, for correction, for instruction in righteousness, that the man of God may be complete, thoroughly equipped for every good work"* (2 Timothy 3:16-17).

As followers of Christ, we are being conformed to His character, so we would do well to be diligent in the reading and study of the Bible. Then we need to expend effort in dependence on the Holy Spirit to live out what we have discovered.

Believe the promises of God – not just for others or as a good principle – but truly yours as a birthright of a child of God. Don't wait to feel as though they are true. Forget feelings for a time and just live in the fact that God has promised and that He is not a liar.

"Trust in the LORD with all your heart, and lean not on your own understanding; in all your ways acknowledge Him, and He shall direct your paths" (Proverbs 3:5-6).

In addition to general guidance through the Scriptures to all men, I also believe that God intended for His children to be personally guided by the Holy Spirit.

"I will instruct you and teach you in the way you should go; I will guide you with My eye. Do not be like the horse or like the mule, which have no understanding, which must be harnessed with bit and bridle, else they will not come near you" (Psalm 32:8-9).

Does He have a plan for my life? What about the decisions that I need to make every day? Will God guide me in these too? Do my daily decisions really matter to a God that has seven billion other people in the world to think about?

Yes, I think He does care and is more than willing to give guidance. *"Therefore humble yourselves under the mighty hand of God, that He may exalt you in due time, casting all your care upon Him, for He cares for you" (1 Peter 5:6-7).* Because God is omnipotent, omniscient, and omnipresent, the number of people in this world is of little consequence to His care for the individual. He is infinite. Because the Holy Spirit lives within you, He is already involved in every aspect of your life.

"I beseech you therefore, brethren, by the mercies of God, that you present your bodies a living sacrifice, holy, acceptable to God, which is your reasonable service. And do not be conformed to this world, but be transformed by the renewing of your mind, that you may prove what is that good and acceptable and perfect will of God" (Romans 12:1-2).

"For we are His workmanship, created in Christ Jesus for good works, which God prepared beforehand that we should walk in them" (Ephesians 2:10).

Although God has certain plans for our lives as illustrated by the above verses, He does not expect us to play some spiritual guessing game looking for a sign from God about what path we should take. He wants us to fully understand His will for us and to embrace it with joy, knowing that it is the good and acceptable and perfect will of God.

So how does the Holy Spirit guide us? First of all, we can have utmost confidence that the Holy Spirit will never lead us to do something contrary to the Bible. In any decision that we make, the first question that we ask ourselves is: "Is this course of action according to the principles of God's word?" If the answer is "no" then we don't need to ask God for further light.

Personal guidance is very much dependent on your relationship with God. If you are walking by the Spirit, you can count on God to guide and direct you on both large and small decisions. He is faithful to you. He is not a deadbeat Dad who abandons His child or fails to provide what His child needs. When He accepted us as His own, He pledged to care for us forever and to nourish us physically, spiritually, and emotionally. *"For as many as are led by the Spirit of God, these are sons of God" (Romans 8:14).*

> *Personal guidance is very much dependent on your relationship with God. If you are walking by the Spirit, you can count on God to guide and direct you on both large and small decisions.*

For smaller decisions, I simply think it is wise to invite the Holy Spirit into the decision. We have a marvelous promise in James chapter 1 that if we ask God for wisdom and believe that He gives it, we will have wisdom.

So I use that repeatedly throughout the day. Before I go into a store, I ask God to give me wisdom regarding the purchases that I will make. When giving counsel to another believer, I ask God to guide the conversation. When I wake up in the morning, I think through the day ahead asking for wisdom for the various situations that I will face. But once I have invited the Holy Spirit to give me wisdom, I don't agonize over the decisions that come from that. I simply pray and then expect the Holy Spirit to guide me through the thoughts that come to mind. It is very low-key. I remember that few decisions are irreversible. Yes, we are to be good stewards of God's resources, and that is why I pray. However, we are not to be emotionally shackled by that responsibility. Don't make little decisions into big ones. Not all decisions are equal. If I buy the wrong kind of bread or a shirt that doesn't look good, the world will not quit turning on its axis.

For bigger decisions, the process requires a bit more investment of time and prayer. I want to make sure that nothing is hindering the Holy Spirit from guiding my thinking. I need to draw near to God and invite Him to search my heart and reveal if there is unconfessed sin there.

Our responsibility is to invite the Holy Spirit into our discerning process. *"Bow down Your ear to me, deliver me speedily; be my rock of refuge, a fortress of defense to save me. For You are my rock and my fortress; therefore, for Your name's sake, lead me and guide me"* (Psalm 31:2-3).

We must be willing to obey all that the Holy Spirit reveals to us. Then we continue to pray and wait on the Lord to bring clarity. God is creative. He can confirm a decision in many different ways: a verse of Scripture, doing a pro and con analysis, the counsel of godly people, open or closed doors, or a settled conviction in my heart about the right course of action. A settled conviction is the opposite of a hyped-up, desperate hoping. I need to be sensitive to the "checks" in my spirit. If I sense a "slow down" or "stop" in my heart, I should not push through with my own desires. Checks are put there by the Holy Spirit to spare me messes and make me wise, but only if I obey them. The Holy Spirit won't continue to warn me if I ignore them. Give God time to direct your thinking, but don't get paralyzed in making a decision.

When you have made your decision, move forward confident that God has led. Usually after committing to the right course of action, peace will be the result. If after making a decision anxiety continues to reign, recheck your thinking before the Lord. Perhaps you missed something.

Be confident that God will continue to work in your life regardless of where you live, who you marry, or what job you took. No decision is fatal in your relationship with Christ. He can redeem even bad choices. *"For this is God, our God forever and ever; he will be our guide even to death"* (Psalm 48:14).

What about when God doesn't seem to speak? What about when you have been praying about a situation and it seems that your prayers are getting no higher than the ceiling? What then? What about when it seems like God is ignoring you or, worse yet, hanging you out to dry?

At that point, you need to reassess the relationship. Are you trusting God? Or accusing Him? Is there sin in your life? Ask Him. If the relationship is fresh, then keep trusting, keep waiting, and continue to worship. Rest in the fact of God's promises. He will eventually lead.

If your relationship is distant – if you doubt His love or His care or His goodness – you need to refresh your relationship with your heavenly Father before expecting personal guidance. You need to seek God for Himself, not simply the answer to your dilemma. You need to familiarize yourself with your Shepherd's voice.

"But he who enters by the door is the shepherd of the sheep. To him the doorkeeper opens, and the sheep hear his voice; and he calls his own sheep by name and leads them out. And when he brings out his own sheep, he goes before them; and the sheep follow him, for they know his voice. Yet they will by no means follow a stranger, but will flee from him, for they do not know the voice of strangers" (John 10:2-5).

If we are grieving, resisting or quenching the Holy Spirit by our own unholy attitudes or actions, guidance and discernment are among the first blessings from God that we lose. Instead of clarity, we have angst. If I am acting apart from the Holy Spirit, I have no spiritual antenna. I haven't paid for that channel on my cable. I am still fleshly-minded and my discernment of spiritual things will suffer.

There was a period in my own life where I had allowed a critical, complaining attitude to invade my life. I was operating mostly in the flesh at that point, trying to do ministry as best as I could. My heart was cold but I didn't fully realize it. I felt like I was justified in my complaining against fellow Christians and that *they* were the problem. I was trying to measure up to the expectations that I thought God had for me. I felt like I needed to earn God's love and work hard to merit His approval. I really didn't get the fact that He forgives abundantly. My spiritual antenna was broken and I didn't even realize it.

I got into a dating relationship with a Christian man, but we weren't good for each other at all. He became hypercritical; I became an angry, frustrated woman. We were constantly applying the wrong spiritual principles to our decisions. We were majorly messed up and didn't see it except that God was on the fringe and we were filled with angst and contradictions. And then we got engaged. We kept hurtling toward the edge of the cliff and would have gotten married except that our pastors refused to marry us because they saw how toxic and ill-conceived the marriage was. How had I gotten so far off track? I had allowed my relationship with Christ to grow stale and be all about works. I was the older brother in the parable of the Prodigal Son. I ignored the Holy Spirit entirely. The spiritual erosion happened over the course of years and getting back to spiritual wholeness took time too. But, although I struggled for a while, God never relinquished His grip on me. He never disinherited me. He will never disinherit you either.

God encourages U-turns. When we repent, He runs to pick up the pieces. He delights in mercy. He will remove the darkness.

God encourages U-turns. When we repent, He runs to pick up the pieces. He delights in mercy. He will remove the darkness.

"Then Jesus spoke to them again, saying, 'I am the light of the world. He who follows Me shall not walk in darkness, but have the light of life'" (John 8:12).

Trust the Lord Jesus to give light through the Holy Spirit. Depend on it.

"Nevertheless I am continually with You; you hold me by my right hand. You will guide me with Your counsel, and afterward receive me to glory" (Psalm 73:23-24).

12

The Holy Spirit Prays for Us

"Likewise the Spirit also helps in our weaknesses. For we do not know what we should pray for as we ought, but the Spirit Himself makes intercession for us with groanings which cannot be uttered. Now He who searches the hearts knows what the mind of the Spirit is, because He makes intercession for the saints according to the will of God…It is Christ who died, and furthermore is also risen, who is even at the right hand of God, who also makes intercession for us" (Romans 8:26-27, 34).

When I was a missionary in Russia, I was very privileged to have a woman in the state of Washington named Doris Templeton praying for me. Doris had MS and was confined to a wheelchair most of the time. Because other avenues of ministry were closed to her, she focused all her effort in praying for "her missionaries." Frequently I would get letters from Doris, and she would write specifically how she was praying for me. Many times she would be praying for something that I thought only God and I knew about. When I was aware that Doris was praying, I was much more confident and bold in my ministry because I knew she had the "ear" of God. Doris lived to pray for her missionaries.

But did you know that you, too, have two ardent prayer warriors praying for you like that? *"Therefore He* [Jesus] *is also able to save to the uttermost those who come to God through Him, since He always lives to make intercession for them" (Hebrews 7:25).*

As if that wasn't sufficient, the word in the Greek New Testament describing what the Holy Spirit does includes the idea that He "over and above" intercedes for us (Strong's Concordance). How incredible is the thought that both the Holy Spirit and Jesus the Son of God are pleading for us before the Father!

The Spirit *"helps us in our weaknesses."* The idea of this phrase is that the Spirit comes alongside to help carry a burden by picking up the other end of the thing that is too heavy for us. It is like when you are trying to move something by yourself and you end up half dragging it because you can't quite muscle the thing. Then someone who is strong comes along and grabs the other end and because he is so much stronger he practically carries the whole thing himself. That is what the Spirit does for us in our praying.

We often feel overwhelmed in situations. We don't know how we ought to pray. We don't know what would please God. We feel confused and conflicted. Some situations are so overwhelming that we can only cry out to God for His mercy and help. When we are most vulnerable, God is not distant. Rather, He is attentively praying for us.

The Spirit comes near in our weakness and prays to the Father with perfect ease and understanding of our situation. *"How precious also are Your thoughts to me, O God! How great is the sum of them! If I should count them, they would be more in number than the sand; when I awake, I am still with You" (Psalm 139:17-18).* Our prayers are muddled messes, but His prayers are right on target.

> *The Spirit comes near in our weakness and prays to the Father with perfect ease and understanding of our situation.*

The Spirit doesn't need words to communicate with God the Father. He simply sighs without spoken words and God the Father, who knows the mind of the Spirit, comprehends exactly what the Spirit is communicating on our behalf. The whole Godhead is working together for the sake of the saints! Wow!

The Spirit makes intercession for the saints according to the will of God. *"Now this is the confidence that we have in Him, that if we ask anything according to His will, He hears us. And if we know that He hears us, whatever we ask, we know that we have the petitions that we have asked of Him"* (1 John 5:14-15).

So the super-charged, right-on-target prayers of the Holy Spirit on our behalf will always be answered with a resounding YES! Whatever the Holy Spirit or Jesus prays for us will be heard by the Father and granted. What a tremendous privilege we possess of having the Holy Spirit and Jesus pleading to God on our behalf.

Because we don't hear those prayers with our ears, we really don't know what Jesus and the Holy Spirit are asking for. But we can be confident that those prayers are good because God is good. We can be assured that they are for our best. The Bible does give some examples of Jesus' prayers for His disciples, and we can logically assume that what He has prayed for others whom He loves, He prays for us whom He loves.

In John chapter 17, we read the prayer of Jesus for the disciples and those who would believe after them. Jesus prayed: *"Holy Father, keep through Your name those whom You have given Me, that they may be one as We are...But now I come to You, and these things I speak in the world, that they may have My joy fulfilled in themselves...I do not pray that You should take them out of the world, but that You should keep them from the evil one. They are not of the world, just as I am not of the world. Sanctify them by Your truth. Your word is truth. As You sent Me into the world, I also have sent them into the world. And for their sakes I sanctify Myself, that they also may be sanctified by the truth. I do not pray for these alone, but also for those who will believe in Me through their word; that they all may be one, as You, Father, are in Me, and I in You; that they also may be one in Us, that the world may believe that You sent Me. And the glory which You gave Me I have given them, that they may be one just as We are one...Father, I desire that they also whom You gave Me may be with Me where I am, that they may behold My glory which You have given Me; for You loved Me before the foundation of the world"* (John 17:11,13,15-22, 24).

In Luke 22:31-34 Jesus prays for Peter, who is in a crisis moment. *"And the Lord said, 'Simon, Simon! Indeed, Satan has asked for you, that he may sift you as wheat. But I have prayed for you, that your faith should not fail; and when you have returned to Me, strengthen your brethren.' But he said to Him, 'Lord, I am ready to go with You, both to prison and to death.' Then He said, 'I tell you, Peter, the rooster shall not crow this day before you will deny three times that you know Me.'"*

Peter is going to face the greatest temptation of his life. Jesus knows it. Jesus knows that Peter is going to fail that test miserably. And so Jesus has prayed for Peter. He prays that Peter's faith will not fail. Here the Greek word that Jesus uses is the word for "cease or die" (Strong's Concordance). He knows that Peter's faith will falter. Peter is trusting in his own devotion and good intentions. Peter is confident that he won't fail. He is sure that he won't abandon Jesus in His time of need. But Peter needs to learn not to trust in himself but in God. Jesus prays that his faith will not die out. And that prayer is answered. Peter denies Jesus three times. But unlike Judas, who hangs himself after regretting what he has done, Peter is restored to fellowship with Jesus in three days. God is not done with Peter and so he is being prayed for.

God Himself creates a safety net for us in prayer. In our scary situations we may feel like we are falling over the edge, but Jesus is praying that we do not fail.

Knowing that the Holy Spirit and Jesus are praying for me should give me courage and boldness in dangerous or overwhelming situations. *"I can do all things through Christ who strengthens me" (Philippians 4:13).* That knowledge should cause me to persevere in trials and temptations because God Himself is pulling for me to resist the temptation and have victory. I will have less fear and more joy. I won't lose heart at the first moment of weakness. Although I acknowledge my weakness, I trust in His sufficiency.

As I comprehend how much Jesus and the Holy Spirit are helping me in prayer, I will see answers to prayer that will thrill my soul. My relationship with God will be deepened as I experience fellowship with the Holy Spirit and Jesus in the secret place of prayer. I will be able to step out in faith more and trust Him for all things that come into my life. *"He who dwells in the secret place of the Most High shall abide under the shadow of the Almighty. I will say of the LORD, 'He is my refuge and my fortress; my God, in Him I will trust'" (Psalm 91:1-2).*

13

The Holy Spirit Strengthens Us

"That He would grant you, according to the riches of His glory, to be strengthened with might through His Spirit in the inner man" (Ephesians 3:16).

Paul is in a prison in Rome writing to a church in whom he had invested more than two years of missionary endeavor. He wanted them to know that he was praying for them and hadn't forgotten them. He asked the Lord to strengthen them in the inner man. He wanted them to have the strength not to give up and to persevere despite hardships. He wanted them to have the inner strength to stand for truth and not crumble under pressure. He wanted them to have the resolve to resist temptation and do what is right.

Battles are more often won by the strength of the inner man than the outer man. When we pray and persevere, God provides mental, moral, spiritual, and physical strength sufficient for (and often surpassing) the need. *"Be of good courage, and He shall strengthen your heart, all you who hope in the LORD"(Psalm 31:24).*

Paul's prayer for the Ephesians reminds them that they are strengthened by faith in the indwelling Christ. *"For this reason I bow my knees to the Father of our Lord Jesus Christ, from whom the whole family in heaven and earth is named, that He would grant you, according to the riches of His glory, to be strengthened with might through His Spirit in the inner man, that Christ may dwell in your hearts through faith; that you, being rooted and grounded in love, may be able to comprehend with all the saints what is the width and length and depth and height--to know the love of Christ which passes knowledge; that you may be filled with all the fullness of God. Now to Him who is able to do exceedingly abundantly above all that we ask or think, according to the power that works in us, to Him be glory in the church by Christ Jesus to all generations, forever and ever. Amen"* (Ephesians 3:14-21).

I wish we would pray that way for one another. Believers in Jesus Christ desperately need to be strong in the inner man. Too often we surrender to sin and the fear of man with hardly any fight at all. We forget that our Lord promises to fight for us.

"For what the law could not do in that it was weak through the flesh, God did by sending His own Son in the likeness of sinful flesh, on account of sin: He condemned sin in the flesh, that the righteous requirement of the law might be fulfilled in us who do not walk according to the flesh but according to the Spirit" (Romans 8:3-4).

Strength comes from being secure in God's love for us. We won't appropriate and seek all that the Lord has provided for us if we are not sure that He really loves us or cares for us. When we learn to rely on God's strength in the difficult times in life, we will find that we receive even more than strength; we will find that the Holy Spirit takes away our fear and gives us peace. *"The LORD will give strength to His people; the LORD will bless His people with peace"* (Psalm 29:11).

In the Old Testament, Samson was a man endowed by God with phenomenal physical strength. However, his inner man was weak. Although a Nazirite who was supposed to be holy and set apart for the Lord, Samson never seemed to cultivate a relationship with God. As a result, he was not able to be all that God desired him to be as a judge of the nation of Israel and died in disgrace at a relatively young age.

God's promises of strength are very personal. His strength resides in Himself. It is not a package that He sends via Fed Ex. He is personally with us through the Holy Spirit. Because of this, we have the resolve to go on with courage and grace and not give in. *"God is our refuge and strength, a very present help in trouble" (Psalm 46:1).*

I love the idea that God is our shelter – the place we can go when we feel vulnerable and afraid. But we don't go to the shelter to cower in fear. We go there to receive strength and to find help in time of need. Our God is a "very present" help in trouble. Because the Holy Spirit is ever present in us, none of our troubles escape His notice. He is always ready to provide help and strength to our inner man.

When we are weak in ourselves, we are perfectly positioned to receive strength from the Lord by the Holy Spirit. *"And lest I should be exalted above measure by the abundance of the revelations, a thorn in the flesh was given to me, a messenger of Satan to buffet me, lest I be exalted above measure. Concerning this thing I pleaded with the Lord three times that it might depart from me. And He said to me, 'My grace is sufficient for you, for My strength is made perfect in weakness.' Therefore most gladly I will rather boast in my infirmities, that the power of Christ may rest upon me. Therefore I take pleasure in infirmities, in reproaches, in needs, in persecutions, in distresses, for Christ's sake. For when I am weak, then I am strong" (2 Corinthians 12:7-10).*

> *When we are weak in ourselves, we are perfectly positioned to receive strength from the Lord by the Holy Spirit.*

When we have given up on our own abilities and strength, then God can fill us with His abundant resources. *"But we have this treasure in earthen vessels, that the excellence of the power may be of God and not of us. We are hard pressed on every side, yet not crushed; we are perplexed, but not in despair; persecuted, but not forsaken; struck down, but not destroyed--always carrying about in the body the dying of the Lord Jesus, that the life of Jesus also may be manifested in our body" (2 Corinthians 4:7-10).*

I remember one evening when I was feeling really rough and weak but needed to go down to the university campus to teach a Bible study. I called a friend and asked her to pray for me. Then I got in my car and started the five-mile drive to campus. By the time I had parked my car at Cleveland State University I was feeling perfectly fine, strong, and clear-headed. The Holy Spirit did that for me.

"Have you not known? Have you not heard? The everlasting God, the LORD, the Creator of the ends of the earth, neither faints nor is weary. His understanding is unsearchable. He gives power to the weak, and to those who have no might He increases strength" (Isaiah 40:28-29).

Unfortunately, in the weakness of our inner man, we often bail out before we discover the strength of the Lord. *"Thus says the LORD: 'Cursed is the man who trusts in man and makes flesh his strength, whose heart departs from the LORD. For he shall be like a shrub in the desert, and shall not see when good comes, but shall inhabit the parched places in the wilderness, in a salt land which is not inhabited. Blessed is the man who trusts in the LORD, and whose hope is the LORD. For he shall be like a tree planted by the waters, which spreads out its roots by the river, and will not fear when heat comes; but its leaf will be green, and will not be anxious in the year of drought, nor will cease from yielding fruit'" (Jeremiah 17:5-8).*

When I was in middle school I ran semi-long distances. My race was 1320 meters – three laps around the track. I ran for several years, but only one race sticks out clearly in my mind because of the lesson in perseverance that I learned that day. I came from a small rural school and we didn't often go to big meets. But one year we went to a bigger meet with schools much larger than mine. I was running the 1320 against some much faster runners. By the end of the second lap I was exhausted. My pace slowed. I thought about quitting. I was out of my league and I knew it. But I kept running because I was certain that my coach would chew me out if I quit. I crossed the line fifth, and to my surprise and delight, I won a ribbon. I ended up being one of only a few on my team that had received a medal or ribbon. Failure had been turned into triumph because I didn't quit when I thought I had nothing left.

The Holy Spirit wants to strengthen us so that we don't give up and don't give in when faced with temptation and difficult situations. The stakes are far higher than a middle school ribbon.

"Therefore we do not lose heart. Even though our outward man is perishing, yet the inward man is being renewed day by day. For our light affliction, which is but for a moment, is working for us a far more exceeding and eternal weight of glory, while we do not look at the things which are seen, but at the things which are not seen. For the things which are seen are temporary, but the things which are not seen are eternal" (2 Corinthians 4:16-18).

Victory and strength will come if we don't give up too soon. God still has good things in store for you. Seek Him. Trust Him with your weakness and appeal to His good care for you. *"My flesh and my heart fail; but God is the strength of my heart and my portion forever"* (Psalm 73:26).

14

The Holy Spirit Gives Wisdom and Discernment

"But as it is written: 'Eye has not seen, nor ear heard, nor have entered into the heart of man the things which God has prepared for those who love Him.' But God has revealed them to us through His Spirit. For the Spirit searches all things, yes, the deep things of God" (1 Corinthians 2:9-10).

The followers of Christ should be people of wisdom, especially when they are filled with the Holy Spirit. *"However, when He, the Spirit of truth, has come, He will guide you into all truth; for He will not speak on His own authority, but whatever He hears He will speak; and He will tell you things to come" (John 16:13).*

We have been given the Holy Spirit to help us to understand the Bible but also to apply it in every area of our lives. *"If any of you lacks wisdom, let him ask of God, who gives to all liberally and without reproach, and it will be given to him. But let him ask in faith, with no doubting, for he who doubts is like a wave of the sea driven and tossed by the wind. For let not that man suppose that he will receive anything from the Lord; he is a double-minded man, unstable in all his ways" (James 1:5-8).*

The Holy Spirit gives us the ability to see life as it really is. Spiritual discernment helps us to untangle the web of half-truths and misapplied information. Discernment will enable us to have a spiritual equilibrium and not be tossed to and fro with every new teaching.

The Holy Spirit also reveals the truth in our own hearts and guards us from self-deception. Too often I hear Bible teachers claim that we can't know our own hearts and that self-deception is inevitable. That is true for unbelievers, but it is a different situation for those who are filled with the Spirit. They use the passage from Jeremiah 17:9: *"The heart is deceitful above all things, and desperately wicked; who can know it?"* But the very next verse tells us that there is One who knows our hearts intimately and without mistake. *"I, the LORD, search the heart, I test the mind, even to give every man according to his ways, according to the fruit of his doings."*

Since the Lord has promised to give us wisdom if we ask for it, we can know our own hearts. The Lord will reveal it to us. *"Search me, O God, and know my heart; try me, and know my anxieties; and see if there is any wicked way in me, and lead me in the way everlasting"(Psalm 139:23-24).*

"For the LORD gives wisdom; from His mouth come knowledge and understanding; He stores up sound wisdom for the upright; he is a shield to those who walk uprightly; He guards the paths of justice, and preserves the way of His saints. Then you will understand righteousness and justice, equity and every good path. When wisdom enters your heart, and knowledge is pleasant to your soul, discretion will preserve you; understanding will keep you" (Proverbs 2:6-11).

In 1 Kings chapter 3, the Lord tells Solomon to ask Him for whatever he wishes. Solomon responds, *"Now, O LORD my God, You have made Your servant king instead of my father David, but I am a little child; I do not know how to go out or come in. And Your servant is in the midst of Your people whom You have chosen, a great people, too numerous to be numbered or counted. Therefore give to Your servant an understanding heart to judge Your people, that I may discern between good and evil. For who is able to judge this great people of Yours?" (1 Kings 3:7-9).*

Solomon desired to be able to discern between good and evil, between truth and half-truth. This thing pleased the Lord. The Lord will be pleased when we, like Solomon, admit our need for greater understanding.

Soon after the Lord gave King Solomon wisdom, two women appeared in his court. Between them they had two infants born only three days apart. One of the children had died in the night and now both women were claiming that the living child was their own. There were no witnesses. It was a classic your-word-against-mine case. With the wisdom that God had given him, Solomon cleverly determines who the real mother is by threatening to divide the living child with a sword. The real mother has mercy on the child while the other woman does not.

Many times we need similar wisdom from the Lord as we apply biblical truth. For example, does a friend who is remorseful for her sin of premarital sex that has led to a pregnancy need further correction or assurances of the forgiveness of the Lord?

Is the person asking for bus fare really going to go on the bus, or is he trying to gather enough funds for a cheap bottle of wine? As we are sensitive to the Holy Spirit and asking for wisdom, He will enable us to discern the situation and apply the appropriate biblical principles. As we are dependent on the Holy Spirit to give discernment, we can interact with individuals whose issues may go far beyond what we are familiar with.

The second chapter of 1 Corinthians describes the wisdom that the Spirit gives to those whom He indwells. *"However, we speak wisdom among those who are mature, yet not the wisdom of this age, nor of the rulers of this age, who are coming to nothing. But we speak the wisdom of God in a mystery, the hidden wisdom which God ordained before the ages for our glory, which none of the rulers of this age knew; for had they known, they would not have crucified the Lord of glory.*

But as it is written: 'Eye has not seen, nor ear heard, nor have entered into the heart of man the things which God has prepared for those who love Him.' But God has revealed them to us through His Spirit. For the Spirit searches all things, yes, the deep things of God. For what man knows the things of a man except the spirit of the man which is in him? Even so no one knows the things of God except the Spirit of God.

Now we have received, not the spirit of the world, but the Spirit who is from God, that we might know the things that have been freely given to us by God. These things we also speak, not in words which man's wisdom teaches but which the Holy Spirit teaches, comparing spiritual things with spiritual. But the natural man does not receive the things of the Spirit of God, for they are foolishness to him; nor can he know them, because they are spiritually discerned.

But he who is spiritual judges all things, yet he himself is rightly judged by no one.

For 'who has known the mind of the Lord that he may instruct Him?' But we have the mind of Christ" (1 Corinthians 2:6-16).

The wisdom that the Holy Spirit gives us is not the wisdom of the world. This is not the wisdom that says I must look out for only my own interests. God's wisdom will not make sense to those who are not followers of Christ because it is often the exact opposite of what the world cherishes.

God reveals His precious truths to His children through the Spirit of God. Since He knows us better than we know ourselves, He is able to communicate with us. He is not hindered by our slowness but will work with us until we understand.

> *God reveals His precious truths to His children through the Spirit of God. He is not hindered by our slowness but will work with us until we understand.*

The Spirit lets us know what God has given us so that we may partake of it. What good would it be for God to give us gifts if we failed to receive them? Often many Christians act as though they are spiritual paupers, forgotten and rejected by God. Oh that they would know the excellencies of Christ which have been given to them and walk in delight of them!

We have the mind of Christ because we have His Spirit indwelling us. Even if we don't understand and appropriate all of it, it's clear that we have far more advantages and wisdom than we utilize. There is so much more resource and sufficiency in Christ than the average Christian even begins to tap. Paul asserts in 1 Corinthians that even the least-esteemed people in the church are better equipped to judge a dispute between believers than secular courts. Why? Because they receive wisdom from God and unbelievers do not.

"Happy is the man who finds wisdom, and the man who gains understanding; for her proceeds are better than the profits of silver, and her gain than fine gold. She is more precious than rubies, and all the things you may desire cannot compare with her" (Proverbs 3:13-15).

SECTION TWO:

Freedom in Christ

15

Letting Go of the Lies

"I beseech you therefore, brethren, by the mercies of God, that you present your bodies a living sacrifice, holy, acceptable to God, which is your reasonable service. And do not be conformed to this world, but be transformed by the renewing of your mind, that you may prove what is that good and acceptable and perfect will of God" (Romans 12:1-2).

Understanding what God the Holy Spirit does for us as believers is vital to a satisfying Christian experience. But true freedom in Christ also requires renewing our minds from lies and misconceptions that have crept into our thinking about God and about ourselves. The first half of this book was focused on how to be holy. The second half concerns our freedom in Christ by finding the truth about God and about ourselves as His children.

All of us know what it is like to not be free. We've carried the feelings of being a loser or of not being good enough or not measuring up. We've carried the scars of abuse – verbal abuse, emotional abuse, physical abuse, sexual abuse. We've felt betrayed by those who should have protected us. We've looked at our circumstances and doubted whether God really loves us. We've doubted that He is for us. We've doubted His forgiveness. We have been overwhelmed by anxiety and fear and the darkness of depression. We have been ensnared by sin. We have rebelled against God. We have gone our own way with disastrous results. Yes, we know what it is to carry baggage.

One of Satan's lies is to make you feel like you are the only one who has spiritual owies. He will try to convince you that everyone else has got life together and that only you struggle. Don't believe it.

One of Satan's lies is to make you feel like you are the only one who has spiritual owies. He will try to convince you that everyone else has got life together and that only you struggle. Don't believe it. What we see on the outside of an individual may have little in common with what is going on in his heart.

The book of James lays out the choice that we have. *"Therefore submit to God. Resist the devil and he will flee from you. Draw near to God and He will draw near to you"* (James 4:7-8a). Every time we are hurting, we must choose which way we are going to run. We can run toward God and find grace and mercy to help in time of need, or we can refuse His embrace and run away.

When we accept and affirm the accusations that we are worthless and not worthy of love, we are not resisting the devil but rather inviting him to set up shop in our hearts. But we are resisting God, His comfort, and His love. Instead of affirming the lies of the accuser, we need to neutralize them with the truth of God.

"Behold, You desire truth in the inward parts, and in the hidden part You will make me to know wisdom. Purge me with hyssop, and I shall be clean; wash me, and I shall be whiter than snow" (Psalm 51:6-7).

The sin in the people around us can cripple us emotionally. But it doesn't have to. What people have done to us isn't who we are. In Christ we have infinite value. We do not have to own that hurt and decay. Abuse and lack of affirmation are things done to you, but they are not you. No parent or spiritual leader is infallible. Every single one of them still has a sin nature and – at times – they will blow it. They will tell us things that are not true.

Will you believe the word of a fallen, selfish human being who, out of his own hurt and feelings of inferiority, has told you that you are not good enough, a failure, insignificant?

Or will you believe the word of Your Savior who gave His life for you and who cannot lie? Will you accept the words of God over your circumstances, over what you have been told, over what you feel? Over the disappointments and trials in your life? Over the deep insecurities that you carry?

We have intrinsic value because we were created in the image of God. True, that image has been marred by sin. However, when we received Christ as Savior, the Holy Spirit began a reclamation and renewal process that will continue until we meet Jesus face-to-face.

Jesus is faithful and just to cleanse us of all unrighteousness – that which we did ourselves and that which was done to us. We do not have to carry the shame of someone else's sin. We don't have to own it; we must not own it.

The God who loves you is perfectly equipped to deal with your spiritual owies if you will receive His love and grace. Trust Him to take your broken places and reshape them and heal them. Take God at His word. He can be trusted with your heart.

"The Spirit of the Lord GOD is upon Me, because the LORD has anointed Me to preach good tidings to the poor; he has sent Me to heal the brokenhearted, to proclaim liberty to the captives, and the opening of the prison to those who are bound; to proclaim the acceptable year of the LORD, and the day of vengeance of our God; to comfort all who mourn, to console those who mourn in Zion, to give them beauty for ashes, the oil of joy for mourning, the garment of praise for the spirit of heaviness; that they may be called trees of righteousness, the planting of the LORD, that He may be glorified" (Isaiah 61:1-3).

16

God's Amazing Love for Us

"Who shall separate us from the love of Christ? Shall tribulation, or distress, or persecution, or famine, or nakedness, or peril, or sword? As it is written: 'For Your sake we are killed all day long; we are accounted as sheep for the slaughter.' Yet in all these things we are more than conquerors through Him who loved us. For I am persuaded that neither death nor life, nor angels nor principalities nor powers, nor things present nor things to come, nor height nor depth, nor any other created thing, shall be able to separate us from the love of God which is in Christ Jesus our Lord" (Romans 8:35-39).

What can make Jesus quit loving you? Not trouble or poverty or persecution. Not angels or demons. Or distance. Or life or death. Or any created thing. Nothing under the sun is going to make Jesus stop loving you.

For much of my first decade and a half as a believer, I had a split personality in regards to the love of God. My head knew the doctrine of the love of God, but my heart treated His love as conditional based on my ability to live up to His standards. If I felt God was pleased with my performance, I was momentarily secure in His love. But if my life or ministry wasn't going well or if I wasn't achieving my goals, I was pretty sure that God was looking down at me with a big, angry frown on His face.

One time when things weren't going well at all, God shouted His love to me and I almost didn't believe Him. I was serving with a missionary team in Russia, but there was going to be a period of three weeks when I would be alone, as both missionary couples were back in the States.

My mind was beset with all kinds of worries – a belligerent, self-righteous man in the church was leveling unfair accusations against the missionaries (and just about anyone else who got in his crosshairs). Also, there was no one to fill the pulpit, and I would be responsible for feeding a temperamental German shepherd guard dog.

As I walked to the store one day, I prayed and poured out my worries to the Lord. I entered a store and noticed that really loud music was pouring from a cassette player on the counter. It sounded like American music, and the only words I could discern were in English. They said, "Jesus loves you. Jesus loves you." I listened intently to try and figure out the rest of the song, but the only words I could pick out were "Jesus loves you. Jesus loves you." Then the shopkeeper walked over and changed the cassette.

At first I dismissed the message as nothing more than a random occurrence. I wasn't expecting God to use an audible voice set to a rock beat to speak to me personally. But as I continued to ponder what had happened, it dawned on me that probably no one else in that store understood the message on that tape. After a while I came to the conclusion that the words were meant just for me as a direct answer to the prayer I'd just sent up to God as I trudged down the street. God was telling me that He loves me and not to be afraid or distressed. He was telling me to hang on and to take courage because His love is sufficient to meet any need.

As I ponder that incident now, 16 years later, I marvel at the power of God to arrange to have that music playing at the precise moment that I walked into that store so burdened over the problems in my life. Although English-language Christian music was not unheard of in Russia at that time, it was rare. Yet I almost missed His declaration of love by writing it off as a coincidence. God is sending us reminders of His love all the time, but sometimes we choose not to receive them.

Because I was never secure in the fact of God's 24/7 love, I was always striving to measure up and earn God's love. I was chasing after an impossible goal. We can never earn God's love.

> *We can never earn God's love. God's love isn't earned, it's given. It overflows from the heart of God to the heart of man.*

God's love isn't earned, it's given. It overflows from the heart of God to the heart of man. From the time of Adam and Eve, humankind has been 100% composed of rebels and enemies of God. There are no exceptions. Not one of us had the ability to ever earn God's love. But God reached out to us in love anyway.

"For God so loved the world that He gave His only begotten Son, that whoever believes in Him should not perish but have everlasting life. For God did not send His Son into the world to condemn the world, but that the world through Him might be saved. He who believes in Him is not condemned; but he who does not believe is condemned already, because he has not believed in the name of the only begotten Son of God. And this is the condemnation, that the light has come into the world, and men loved darkness rather than light, because their deeds were evil" (John 3:16-19).

In love God pursued His enemies – not to punish but to rescue. The Godhead sent Jesus to us to put on a human body and die on the cross to take the punishment that was rightly ours as defiant breakers of God's law. He made the way for us to be reconciled to God. Those that have received Jesus Christ as their Savior have been elevated from the position of enemy and rebel to the position of precious child of God and joint heir with Christ.

"For as many as are led by the Spirit of God, these are sons of God. For you did not receive the spirit of bondage again to fear, but you received the Spirit of adoption by whom we cry out, 'Abba, Father.' The Spirit Himself bears witness with our spirit that we are children of God, and if children, then heirs-- heirs of God and joint heirs with Christ, if indeed we suffer with Him, that we may also be glorified together" (Romans 8:14-17).

Upon receiving forgiveness of sins, we went from outcast, loser, and failure to accepted in the Beloved. The wrath of the Father towards us was completely satisfied. *"But God demonstrates His own love toward us, in that while we were still sinners, Christ died for us. Much more then, having now been justified by His blood, we shall be saved from wrath through Him. For if when we were enemies we were reconciled to God through the death of His Son, much more, having been reconciled, we shall be saved by His life. And not only that, but we also rejoice in God through our Lord Jesus Christ, through whom we have now received the reconciliation" (Romans 5:8-11).* That's tremendously powerful love.

There is nothing I can do to make Jesus love me more; there is nothing I can do to make Him love me less. God's love is extended to us freely, perfectly, infinitely. He can't love half-heartedly.

Unfortunately the phrases "God loves you" and "Jesus died on the cross for you" have become clichés in the minds of Christians and unbelievers alike. We've heard the phrases so many times that it doesn't catch our hearts any more. We need to reclaim the love of God from the cliché pile. It is precious.

God's provision of salvation and His bringing us to faith in Himself should end all discussion of whether God truly loves us, and yet as humans, we need frequent reminders from those we love that they still love us too because our hearts leak and the truth drains out.

"As a father pities his children, so the LORD pities those who fear Him. For He knows our frame; he remembers that we are dust" (Psalm 103:13-14).

As our perfect Heavenly Father, He shows His love to us by pledging Himself to provide everything we need for both life and godliness. We are not helpless orphans or neglected children.

The Father is ever attentive to each of His children having placed within us His Holy Spirit to be our constant companion and guide through the trials and difficulties of life. *"Therefore He is also able to save to the uttermost those who come to God through Him, since He always lives to make intercession for them" (Hebrews 7:25).*

"The LORD is near to all who call upon Him, to all who call upon Him in truth. He will fulfill the desire of those who fear Him; He also will hear their cry and save them" (Psalm 145:18-19).

"Are not five sparrows sold for two copper coins? And not one of them is forgotten before God. But the very hairs of your head are all numbered. Do not fear therefore; you are of more value than many sparrows" (Luke 12:6-7).

"Through the LORD'S mercies we are not consumed, because His compassions fail not. They are new every morning; great is Your faithfulness" (Lamentations 3:22-23).

Jesus was the most compassionate towards the broken, the honest, the tax collector, and the sinner. His sharpest comments were for the Pharisees and His own disciples who weren't hearing or believing what they'd been taught.

"Seeing then that we have a great High Priest who has passed through the heavens, Jesus the Son of God, let us hold fast our confession. For we do not have a High Priest who cannot sympathize with our weaknesses, but was in all points tempted as we are, yet without sin. Let us therefore come boldly to the throne of grace, that we may obtain mercy and find grace to help in time of need" (Hebrews 4:14-16).

God's love does not guarantee a problem-free life of ease. Rather, He promises to go with us through the adventures of life.

"I will love You, O LORD, my strength. The LORD is my rock and my fortress and my deliverer; my God, my strength, in whom I will trust; my shield and the horn of my salvation, my stronghold. I will call upon the LORD, who is worthy to be praised; so shall I be saved from my enemies" (Psalm 18:1-3).

Our God is our safe haven. When we are in a mess or need rescuing, He'll be there. He will not relinquish His grip on us, and nobody can pluck us out of His hand. We are secure regardless of the circumstances. Therefore, we do not need to be afraid or worry or fret. There will be daunting, uncomfortable times, but our God will be right in the midst of them with us.

"You number my wanderings; put my tears into Your bottle; are they not in Your book? When I cry out to You, then my enemies will turn back; this I know, because God is for me. In God (I will praise His word), in the LORD (I will praise His word), in God I have put my trust; I will not be afraid. What can man do to me?" (Psalm 56:8-11).

"God is our refuge and strength, a very present help in trouble. Therefore we will not fear, even though the earth be removed, and though the mountains be carried into the midst of the sea; though its waters roar and be troubled, though the mountains shake with its swelling. Selah" (Psalm 46:1-3).

> *Because God is a very present help in trouble, I can be assured that He knows what is going on and that He cares. He is with me and I am secure.*

Because God is a very present help in trouble, I can be assured that He knows what is going on and that He cares. I am not dependent on my own resources, skills, and efforts. I am not limited by my own frailties, insecurities, and helplessness. I am not on my own. He is with me and I am secure.

In His love He is our protection. *"For the eyes of the LORD run to and fro throughout the whole earth, to show Himself strong on behalf of those whose heart is loyal to Him" (2 Chronicles 16:9a).*

"The angel of the LORD encamps all around those who fear Him, and delivers them. Oh, taste and see that the LORD is good; blessed is the man who trusts in Him!" (Psalm 34:7-8).

As a loving Father He also provides what His children require. He is not indifferent to our needs. *"Grace and peace be multiplied to you in the knowledge of God and of Jesus our Lord, as His divine power has given to us all things that pertain to life and godliness, through the knowledge of Him who called us by glory and virtue, by which have been given to us exceedingly great and precious promises, that through these you may be partakers of the divine nature, having escaped the corruption that is in the world through lust" (2 Peter 1:2-4).*

"Therefore do not worry, saying, 'What shall we eat?' or 'What shall we drink?' or 'What shall we wear?' For after all these things the Gentiles seek. For your heavenly Father knows that you need all these things. But seek first the kingdom of God and His righteousness, and all these things shall be added to you" (Matthew 6:31-33).

I've noticed in my interactions with people that if someone is secure in God's love, he will see evidence of His love everywhere. However if that person doubts His love, he won't see evidence of it anywhere. Let us not be doubters and miss His expressions of divine love.

"But without faith it is impossible to please Him, for he who comes to God must believe that He is, and that He is a rewarder of those who diligently seek Him" (Hebrews 11:6).

Beloved, don't overlook the love moments of God or attribute them to luck. *"Do not be deceived, my beloved brethren. Every good gift and every perfect gift is from above, and comes down from the Father of lights, with whom there is no variation or shadow of turning" (James 1:16-17).*

God is creative in showing His love. We need to pay attention. God's love can be seen in a sunrise or sunset, in the beauty of a flower, in the solution to a problem, or in the hug of a friend. It is evident in the answering of little prayers with tender mercy.

Whether you feel loved or not, respond to God as though He loves you. Expect Him to love you rather than doubting that fact. Look for

God's demonstrations of His love for you as an individual and praise Him for them. As you pray, go to Him as an especially loved child would go to his earthly father with requests. *"In that day you will ask in My name, and I do not say to you that I shall pray the Father for you; for the Father Himself loves you, because you have loved Me, and have believed that I came forth from God" (John 16:26-27).*

Be specific in prayer but open-handed, allowing God to answer in His own way. Praise Him for the love moments no matter how small. Seek God as a Person, not just for what He gives you.

In response to His sacrificial love, love Him back. *"I have been crucified with Christ; it is no longer I who live, but Christ lives in me; and the life which I now live in the flesh I live by faith in the Son of God, who loved me and gave Himself for me" (Galatians 2:20).*

Love for God shows itself in obedience to His commands and love for His children. *"And we have known and believed the love that God has for us. God is love, and he who abides in love abides in God, and God in him. Love has been perfected among us in this: that we may have boldness in the day of judgment; because as He is, so are we in this world. There is no fear in love; but perfect love casts out fear, because fear involves torment. But he who fears has not been made perfect in love. We love Him because He first loved us. If someone says, 'I love God,' and hates his brother, he is a liar; for he who does not love his brother whom he has seen, how can he love God whom he has not seen? And this commandment we have from Him: that he who loves God must love his brother also" (I John 4:16-21).*

"As the Father loved Me, I also have loved you; abide in My love. If you keep My commandments, you will abide in My love, just as I have kept My Father's commandments and abide in His love. These things I have spoken to you, that My joy may remain in you, and that your joy may be full. This is My commandment, that you love one another as I have loved you. Greater love has no one than this, than to lay down one's life for his friends" (John 15:9-13).

17

Abundantly Forgiven

"Let the wicked forsake his way, and the unrighteous man his thoughts; let him return to the LORD, and He will have mercy on him; and to our God, for He will abundantly pardon" (Isaiah 55:7).

When I was a new Christian just beginning to understand the grace of God, I was asked to help drive the youth of my church to an ice skating event in another town two hours away. Pastor Dan Minyard gave me very clear instructions that I was to go and pick up a certain kid at his house and then meet up with the pastor and the rest of the group at a particular location. Then we would drive together in a caravan to the event. I was specifically told not to drive on ahead without the rest of the group.

So I and the people in my vehicle headed to the house of the kid we were picking up. But half way there, we saw him driving the other way, so we turned around and headed to the spot where I thought we were meeting the pastor. We parked where I assumed the meeting place was. By this time it was raining hard and the windows of my car were fogging up. We thought we saw the pastor's car go past, so we took off after him. We followed him up the mountain pass and then realized that it wasn't him. This was in the days before cell phones.

We waited at the top of the pass hoping that the pastor would catch up with us. He didn't. So we finally started toward our destination in Walla Walla, WA. Just before we got to Walla Walla, the other vehicle caught up with us and we followed them to the ice rink.

I knew that I was about to get chewed out. And I thoroughly deserved it. I had done the very thing that I was specifically told not to do. But when we got to the rink Pastor Minyard asked me if everyone was all right. I said, "Yes." He said something to the effect of, "Praise the Lord everyone's OK." He didn't yell at me. He didn't demand an explanation. He just forgave me. And that was the end of the matter. I was flabbergasted. I couldn't think of another time where someone who had every right to yell at me and nail me to the wall didn't do it. But that, beloved, is an example of what Jesus Christ does for us every day.

God's remedy for our sin is confession. God promises over and over in the Scriptures that if we will turn in repentance from our sin, He will abundantly forgive and restore our relationship with Him.

"If we confess our sins, He is faithful and just to forgive us our sins and to cleanse us from all unrighteousness" (1 John 1:9).

"And you, being dead in your trespasses and the uncircumcision of your flesh, He has made alive together with Him, having forgiven you all trespasses, having wiped out the handwriting of requirements that was against us, which was contrary to us. And He has taken it out of the way, having nailed it to the cross" (Colossians 2:13-14).

"For I will be merciful to their unrighteousness, and their sins and their lawless deeds I will remember no more" (Hebrews 8:12).

In 1 Corinthians chapter 13 we have a definition of love. Among the characteristics as listed in the New International Version is "keeps no record of wrongs." In the Greek, it is literally "doesn't take an inventory of worthless or injurious things" (Strong's Concordance). God does not keep a record of our wrongs. It is not that He cannot remember them but rather that He chooses not to remember. When He forgives our sin, He no longer holds it against us. It is as if He erases the hard

When we seek forgiveness, God will not hesitate to forgive, even when we repeatedly fail.

drive containing the evidence. When we seek forgiveness, God will not hesitate to forgive, even when we repeatedly fail.

Often times we feel as though Jesus will forgive our mistakes but that repeated sins are in a different category. We know what we should do, but we don't do it. Over and over we complain, or yell at our roommate, or think lustful thoughts and fall into the same pattern of sin. We think that Jesus must certainly get tired of us coming to Him again and again for forgiveness. But Jesus taught His disciples, *"If your brother sins against you, rebuke him; and if he repents, forgive him. And if he sins against you seven times in a day, and seven times in a day returns to you, saying, 'I repent,' you shall forgive him"* (Luke 17:3-4).

True forgiveness means that the offended one will no longer hold the sin against the offender and will no longer bring it up again to anyone else or even to themselves. Therefore, the next time we fail in a similar way, Jesus does not look at the hundred times we've done that before. He sees the current offense as the only one that stands between Him and us.

"I, even I, am He who blots out your transgressions for My own sake; and I will not remember your sins" (Isaiah 43:25).

"Who is a God like You, pardoning iniquity and passing over the transgression of the remnant of His heritage? He does not retain His anger forever, because He delights in mercy. He will again have compassion on us, and will subdue our iniquities. You will cast all our sins into the depths of the sea" (Micah 7:18-19).

When He casts our sins into the depths of the sea they are gone…gone forever! The deepest spot in the ocean is located in the Mariana Trench off the coast of Guam. It is approximately 6.8 miles deep. Anything dropped into that hole is not coming back – ever.

Jesus' love is so immense that He carries the pain of our failures; He refuses to allow our sin to drive a wedge between Himself and us. We need to take God at His word and count ourselves forgiven whether we feel anything or not. Generally, after I've blown it in any particular area and confessed it, I don't feel the guilt lifting. I don't feel a giant sense of relief. I feel stupid for giving in to that particular sin. I still feel remorse. But I don't operate on feelings. I operate on truth despite my feelings and stand on the fact that I am forgiven. After you confess your sin, you are reconciled and things are good between you and God, whether you feel it or not.

Count your sin dealt with. If you continue to beat yourself up and call yourself a lousy Christian, you'll live up to that appraisal. The pattern of sin will continue. But if you rest in the fact that you are forgiven and that your relationship with God has been fully restored, the cycle of sin will be broken. After confession, reckon yourself forgiven and walk in righteousness.

If Satan starts to accuse you of being a loser, don't confirm his accusation. Deny it. Don't affirm all the other times you've done that particular sin, because only the current sin separates you from Christ's fellowship.

Because we know that confession brings unhindered fellowship with Christ, we are wise to open up our whole lives to the searchlight of Christ. He sees it anyway. *"Blessed is he whose transgression is forgiven, whose sin is covered. Blessed is the man to whom the LORD does not impute iniquity, and in whose spirit there is no deceit. When I kept silent, my bones grew old through my groaning all the day long. For day and night Your hand was heavy upon me; my vitality was turned into the drought of summer. Selah I acknowledged my sin to You, and my iniquity I have not hidden. I said, 'I will confess my transgressions to the LORD,' and You forgave the iniquity of my sin. Selah"* (Psalm 32:1-5).

God's forgiveness should lead me to deal with my failures quickly and completely because I know that He is willing to forgive and cleanse me. I keep short accounts with God and sin is dealt with before it gets totally out of control. My heart is tender and responsive to correction because I trust God's love and forgiveness.

I go a step further and invite Christ to show me where there might be something hindering that I am not aware of. *"Search me, O God, and know my heart; try me, and know my anxieties; and see if there is any wicked way in me, and lead me in the way everlasting"* (Psalm 139:23-24).

Only Christ, not Satan or other people, has the authority to condemn us, but He has chosen not to. *"Who shall bring a charge against God's elect? It is God who justifies. Who is he who condemns? It is Christ who died, and furthermore is also risen, who is even at the right hand of God, who also makes intercession for us"* (Romans 8:33-34).

"O wretched man that I am! Who will deliver me from this body of death? I thank God-- through Jesus Christ our Lord! So then, with the mind I myself serve the law of God, but with the flesh the law of sin. There is therefore now

no condemnation to those who are in Christ Jesus, who do not walk according to the flesh, but according to the Spirit" (Romans 7:24-8:1).

I don't have the right to condemn anyone else, even if I see things in their character that are less than godly. With humility I can, and should, address the sin, but God has not given me the authority to condemn them.

"Then Peter came to Him and said, 'Lord, how often shall my brother sin against me, and I forgive him? Up to seven times?' Jesus said to him, 'I do not say to you, up to seven times, but up to seventy times seven'" (Matthew 18:21-22).

Because I know what it is to be completely forgiven, I am to be gracious and forgiving to those who do wrong against me. *"And be kind to one another, tenderhearted, forgiving one another, just as God in Christ forgave you" (Ephesians 4:32).* Christ has forgiven me completely and unreservedly. In exuberant gratefulness, I must pass on that mercy to brothers and sisters in Christ who stumble just like I do. Christ has forgiven me of more than I will ever be required to forgive of someone else.

18

God is Good and Faithful

"The LORD is good to all, and His tender mercies are over all His works" (*Psalm 145:9*).

God is good. We know this, first of all, because God defines Himself this way. *"This is the message which we have heard from Him and declare to you, that God is light and in Him is no darkness at all"* (1 John 1:5).

"Oh, taste and see that the LORD is good; blessed is the man who trusts in Him!" (Psalm 34:8).

"The LORD is good, a stronghold in the day of trouble; and He knows those who trust in Him" (Nahum 1:7).

"Through the LORD'S mercies we are not consumed, because His compassions fail not. They are new every morning; great is Your faithfulness. 'The LORD is my portion,' says my soul, 'Therefore I hope in Him!' The LORD is good to those who wait for Him, to the soul who seeks Him" (Lamentations 3:22-25).

"For the LORD is good; his mercy is everlasting, and His truth endures to all generations" (Psalm 100:5).

God demonstrates His goodness to us with fresh compassion every morning and mercy that goes on for all eternity.

I'd moved to Irkutsk, Siberia, in September 1999 and needed to find an apartment near my coworkers because, from the moment I got off the plane, my health was precarious. I also needed to be relatively close to the State University because I didn't plan on getting a car. As a single person I wanted to rent a one-room apartment; anything larger than that might appear like I was flaunting my comparative wealth as an American. I went to two separate rental agencies and was told that there was absolutely no one-room apartments available for rent in the entire region of Akademgorodok. Students attending the university were renting them all. I was sure God *could* take care of my need but not 100% sure He would take care of it. I almost took an apartment in another region because I was afraid I wouldn't find anything close by.

But then my Russian language teacher told me she had a friend who was looking to rent out a second apartment that she had. Her friend and a neighbor had both lost their spouses and now they had gotten married. They were living in a one-room apartment and had an adjacent three-room apartment to rent out. I rented two rooms of that apartment which turned out to be in the building right next to my coworkers – a mere minute and a half walk away! What looks impossible for man is possible for a good God who cares for His children.

"Yea, though I walk through the valley of the shadow of death, I will fear no evil; for You are with me; your rod and Your staff, they comfort me. You prepare a table before me in the presence of my enemies; you anoint my head with oil; my cup runs over. Surely goodness and mercy shall follow me all the days of my life; and I will dwell in the house of the LORD forever" (Psalm 23:4-6).

Goodness and mercy shall follow after God's people all the days of their lives. When I am walking in obedience to my heavenly Father, I'm going to have goodness and mercy dogging my steps everywhere I go. I will never be far from His kindness.

> *When I am walking in obedience to my heavenly Father, I'm going to have goodness and mercy dogging my steps everywhere I go. I will never be far from His kindness.*

One day I was driving down to Cleveland State University to do a one-on-one Bible study with a female student. My plan was to stop at the bank on the way down to school to get quarters for the parking meter. I knew that I had no change with me. I also knew that there were no stray coins in my car because I had scoured it the day before to pay the meter. So it was essential for me to stop at the bank.

However, when I got to the bank, it was closed. I'd missed it by just a couple of minutes. Knowing that I had no time to try to get change anywhere else, I told the Lord that He knew all about my situation. I asked Him to provide a parking space with a meter with time still on it. And then I drove to CSU. *"I would have lost heart, unless I had believed that I would see the goodness of the LORD in the land of the living. Wait on the LORD; be of good courage, and He shall strengthen your heart; wait, I say, on the LORD!"* (Psalm 27:13-14).

I found a parking space. I got out of the car and looked at the meter. It had 35 minutes on it. At 6 p.m. parking in downtown Cleveland is free. I looked at my cell phone. The time was 5:25 p.m. The Lord had provided a meter with the exact amount of time that I needed on it! His precise provision was such a blessing because it pointed to His faithfulness. He had heard my prayer and gave His daughter exactly what she needed.

"Blessed be the Lord, who daily loads us with benefits, the God of our salvation! Selah" (Psalm 68:19).

Often it is the scary and uncertain situations in our lives that cause us to doubt God's goodness. When we lose our job or suffer a serious injury or some dream that we chased is slipping away, we look at God differently. Loss, in its many forms, makes us wonder why God is good to everyone else but seems to be ignoring us. We look at our circumstances and we don't like what we see. We want our lives to be smooth and problem-free with no speed bumps or detours to slow us down. We want easy.

We blame God and question His goodness because we are hurting. We question His character based on our perceptions of what is fair. We are finite and He is infinite, and yet we accuse God of mismanaging our lives.

"But indeed, O man, who are you to reply against God? Will the thing formed say to him who formed it, 'Why have you made me like this?' Does not the potter have power over the clay, from the same lump to make one vessel for honor and another for dishonor?" (Romans 9:20-21).

We can't define God by our circumstances. We live in a fallen world. Sin has corrupted the world and everything in it. When life seems unfair, that doesn't change the character of God. It is impossible for our changeable circumstances to define the unchangeable character of God.

When we find ourselves in difficult circumstances that seem beyond our ability to bear, we need to refrain from thinking, "IF God is good, why is this happening to me?" but rather think "BECAUSE God is good, He will see me through this circumstance."

"For I consider that the sufferings of this present time are not worthy to be compared with the glory which shall be revealed in us. For the earnest expectation of the creation eagerly waits for the revealing of the sons of God. For the creation was subjected to futility, not willingly, but because of Him who subjected it in hope; because the creation itself also will be delivered from the bondage of corruption into the glorious liberty of the children of God" (Romans 8:18-21).

God's greatest purpose in your life is not your comfort and success. Rather, He desires holiness in your life and to make you like Jesus. Spiritual maturity doesn't happen in a stress-free, problem-free world. *"Therefore let those who suffer according to the will of God commit their souls to Him in doing good, as to a faithful Creator"* (1 Peter 4:19).

God sees the long view and knows what will bring about a character that reflects Him well. Just as a Marine needs to go through boot camp to learn how to be a soldier, so we need to go through trials to produce steadfastness in our walk with Christ. It is in the difficulties that we most see the power and faithfulness of God.

We can trust God to carry us through and to remain with us throughout the difficult time. He has promised not to abandon us. *"For He Himself has said, 'I will never leave you nor forsake you.' So we may boldly say: 'The Lord is my helper; I will not fear. What can man do to me?'"* (Hebrews 13:5b-6).

God is good. He is your protector and He has your back. You are His, and He will never let you go. *"The LORD is your keeper; the LORD is your shade at your right hand. The sun shall not strike you by day, nor the moon by night. The LORD shall preserve you from all evil; he shall preserve your soul. The LORD shall preserve your going out and your coming in from this time forth, and even forevermore"* (Psalm 121:5-8).

19

God is For Us

"What then shall we say to these things? If God is for us, who can be against us? He who did not spare His own Son, but delivered Him up for us all, how shall He not with Him also freely give us all things?" (Romans 8:31-32).

The tone of this passage is intended to be jubilant. The emphasis is not on "if" God is for us. That's not in question because the very next sentence indicates that He was so much for us that He did not spare His own Son but gave Him for our redemption. The passage goes on to inform us that the only One who has the right to condemn us has chosen instead to intercede on our behalf. Nothing can separate us from the love of Christ. Therefore, we are more than conquerors through Him who loves us.

Furthermore, He will also freely give us all things that we require in this life. *"As His divine power has given to us all things that pertain to life and godliness, through the knowledge of Him who called us by glory and virtue, by which have been given to us exceedingly great and precious promises, that through these you may be partakers of the divine nature, having escaped the corruption that is in the world through lust" (2 Peter 1:3-4).*

God is for His children. As a born-again believer, your Heavenly Father is not out to get you. He is not out to deprive you of everything that you care strongly about. And He is not trying to rob you of joy. *"You will show me the path of life; in Your presence is fullness of joy; at Your right hand are pleasures forevermore" (Psalm 16:11).*

Sometimes we forget that. How often do we think that if we want something very much that God is against that desire? Even when God promises us in Psalm 37 that if we delight in Him, He will give us the desires of our heart. Or do we try to beg and plead with God to manipulate Him into helping us with some need, when He invites us in 1 Peter 5:7 to cast *"all your care upon Him, for He cares for you"*?

In some churches, God is depicted as ready to slap us when we step out of line. How often do we testimonies talk about God having to "break" us or God "using a 2 x 4 across our head" to get His point across? Is the expected Christian life one where the believer is in opposition with a distant and strict disciplinarian? No! A thousand times, no.

There is an adversary for believers in the Bible – but it's not God. Satan is the adversary. *"Be sober, be vigilant; because your adversary the devil walks about like a roaring lion, seeking whom he may devour" (1 Peter 5:8).*

"So the great dragon was cast out, that serpent of old, called the Devil and Satan, who deceives the whole world; he was cast to the earth, and his angels were cast out with him. Then I heard a loud voice saying in heaven, 'Now salvation, and strength, and the kingdom of our God, and the power of His Christ have come, for the accuser of our brethren, who accused them before our God day and night, has been cast down'" (Revelation 12:9-10).

The adversary and the accuser are Satan. How wrong of us to attribute to God the very characteristics of the Devil.

Many times believers' relationships with God are patterned after their relationship with their parents, especially their father. If that relationship was not close or if the relationship was dependent on the child's performance, that often translates into a believer relating negatively to God. Know that God is not like the people in your life who have let you down or failed you. God is not like your earthly father – even if you had a great dad. God the Father is unique. Therefore, we need to come to Him as He has defined Himself in the Scriptures.

Read the Bible for yourself, asking the Holy Spirit to show you what God is like and to clear away misconceptions about who He is. Let God Himself, through His Word, tell you what He is like.

To unrepentant unbelievers, He shows the law to reveal their sin to them and bring them to repentance; to the born-again child, He shows grace. When the Father must correct His child, He does it in love and for the child's profit. When we are tempted by sin, God does not turn away. Rather the Holy Spirit jumps to the rescue and provides a way of escape. If we continue to rebel, the Holy Spirit will bring conviction so we can repent and be restored.

Jesus told a story to His disciples to reveal the heart of the Father towards His children – the ones who stumble and fall and the ones who take pride in their conformity to His expectations. It is found in Luke 15:11-32. The younger son demands his inheritance and freedom from his father. And so the father gives him his inheritance and off goes the son to waste it in living according to all his own fleshy desires. He loses all his money and a famine comes to the place where he is staying and the young man is in deep trouble. He's starving and out of options. But then he starts thinking about home and about his dad. His dad treats people well. His dad's hired help have more than enough food. So he decides to take responsibility for his failure and ask for his dad's forgiveness. He knows he's no longer worthy of the title "son," but he hopes his dad will hire him on as a workman on the family farm.

As he heads home his heart is pounding. He's not sure how his dad is going to treat him. He worries that maybe his dad will want nothing to do with him. Maybe his dad will call him a loser and order him off the property. He certainly deserves that.

But while he was still a great way off, he sees someone running in his direction. It looks like his dad; it is his dad! Before the son can quite figure it out, his dad is hugging and kissing him. The son gets halfway through his prepared speech of repentance before his dad cuts him off, calling the workmen to bring out the best set of clothes, shoes, and a ring. His dad proclaims that they will have a welcome home party, a celebration for his safe return. No mention is made of the life that the son has lived, even though the news about him had made it back to the farm. The son had made some really poor decisions, but the father is more concerned that he has come to his senses and finally found his way home.

Our Father does not condemn us as His children. He never writes us off as hopeless losers. *"But to him who does not work but believes on Him who justifies the ungodly, his faith is accounted for righteousness, just as David also describes the blessedness of the man to whom God imputes righteousness apart from works: 'Blessed are those whose lawless deeds are forgiven, and whose sins are covered; blessed is the man to whom the Lord shall not impute sin.'"* (Romans 4:5-8).

The older son was the self-righteous one. He, too, had a skewed image of his father. To the older son, the relationship was all about performance and measuring up to what he felt his father wanted. He refused to go into the party for his no-good brother. He couldn't see why his father would reward such despicable behavior. To him, his brother deserved to rot in hell. The older son had seen the grief of his father every day as he stood and looked down the road, praying that his younger son would come home.

When his father comes out to plead with him to come into the party, the older son is angry and accuses his father of not properly rewarding him for his perfect obedience. The father reminds his older son that he owns all the family's holdings; he could have had any number of celebrations. Being forgiving and grace-filled was who the father was. The older son should have known that.

Two sons – both of whom didn't understand the heart of their father. One who couldn't wait to leave but who ultimately comes back because he realizes what he threw away. One who never left, but never allowed himself to receive the love of his father. One restored. One still standing outside refusing to believe that his father was for him.

The relationship between God and His children is supposed to be an interconnected, mutually beneficial union. *"Abide in Me, and I in you. As the branch cannot bear fruit of itself, unless it abides in the vine, neither can you, unless you abide in Me. I am the vine, you are the branches. He who abides in Me, and I in him, bears much fruit; for without Me you can do nothing"* (John 15:4-5).

The vine nourishes the branch. Jesus desires to flow into us 24/7. It is not an adversarial relationship. The vine protects, feeds, supports, and provides everything that the branch needs to be fruitful. They work together in harmony. Each one is relying on the other to do its part.

God desires that we come to Him with our needs in simple trust and faith – not just for the monumental things, but for the everyday needs of life – because He is for us. After a vacation Bible school at my church, three helium balloons were stuck on the ceiling of the sanctuary. The ceiling was too high to be able to get them down with even our tallest ladder and a reaching pole. Finally, our church intern and I decided to try to get them down by snagging them with duct tape affixed to another helium balloon attached to a long thread. The process sounded simple enough but it was hard to maneuver the balloon using only a thread. After some effort and time, our intern snagged the first balloon and hauled it down. On the second balloon we were having difficulty getting the two balloons to connect. They seemed to keep moving away from each other as soon as they got close.

After quite a bit of fishing and maneuvering I said, "Lord, we could use help here." Instantly, the balloon on the thread drifted over and securely latched on to the errant balloon. It was as if God was saying with a grin, "Sure, I can help you with that. Why didn't you ask me sooner?"

The third balloon was lodged above a huge light fixture. But in a relatively short amount of time, the duct tape on the catching balloon snagged the other balloon by its ribbon! Who could do that but God?

God doesn't desire to be at cross purposes with His children. He is not holding out on them. Oftentimes, He is waiting for us to quit holding out on Him.

> *If God is for us, it doesn't matter who or what is against us. If God is against us, it doesn't matter who is for us.*

If God is for us, it doesn't matter who or what is against us. If God is against us, it doesn't matter who is for us. *"Fear not, for I have redeemed you; I have called you by your name; you are Mine. When you pass through the waters, I will be with you; and through the rivers, they shall not overflow you. When you walk through the fire, you shall not be burned, nor shall the flame scorch you. For I am the LORD your God, the Holy One of Israel, your Savior"* (Isaiah 43:1b-3a).

20

Triumphing Over Feelings of Inadequacy

"Blessed is the man who trusts in the LORD, and whose hope is the LORD. For he shall be like a tree planted by the waters, which spreads out its roots by the river, and will not fear when heat comes; but its leaf will be green, and will not be anxious in the year of drought, nor will cease from yielding fruit" (Jeremiah 17:7-8).

Freedom in Christ is dependent on understanding who God is and in appropriating all that the Holy Spirit does for us. But we also have to face what we believe about ourselves. Some of us struggle deeply with feelings of inadequacy and a fear of not being able to measure up to what a "good" Christian should be.

We are driven – not by the love of God or love to God – but by an intense desire to just not mess it all up. We are haunted by what we are "supposed" to do and "supposed" to accomplish. We focus on all our failures and usually overlook insufficiencies in anyone else. We are sure that anybody else could do a better job of being a Christian than we can and we wonder why God bothers with us at all since we are so flawed.

God our Creator is grieved when His children feel like losers who can never measure up. He does not want us to be defeated and depressed and feel alienated from Him. He has already done everything to make us acceptable in His sight. He has called us, brought us to faith, and redeemed us as His own. He has given us His Holy Spirit and made us the temple of God. *"Do you not know that you are the temple of God and that the Spirit of God dwells in you? If anyone defiles the temple of God, God will destroy him. For the temple of God is holy, which temple you are"* (1 Corinthians 3:16-17).

> *God our Creator is grieved when His children feel like losers who can never measure up.*

He has taken away our sin and exchanged it for the very righteousness of Christ. *"Yet indeed I also count all things loss for the excellence of the knowledge of Christ Jesus my Lord, for whom I have suffered the loss of all things, and count them as rubbish, that I may gain Christ and be found in Him, not having my own righteousness, which is from the law, but that which is through faith in Christ, the righteousness which is from God by faith"* (Philippians 3:8-9).

We can't earn God's favor because we already have it as a gift from Him. *"I have been crucified with Christ; it is no longer I who live, but Christ lives in me; and the life which I now live in the flesh I live by faith in the Son of God, who loved me and gave Himself for me. I do not set aside the grace of God; for if righteousness comes through the law, then Christ died in vain"* (Galatians 2:20-21).

When Christ says that you are good enough, that's the last word. It doesn't matter what somebody else says about you or even what you tell yourself. Because your Savior not only has the authority to declare you sufficient, He also has the ability to pull it off. In response to your need and your prayer He gives strength, patience, wisdom, peace, joy, security, safety, grace, mercy – whatever you need. The grace of God covers over a multitude of our self-perceived deficiencies. If we trust His Presence, we don't need to be afraid of anything because nothing is bigger than He is.

When you received Christ as your Savior, God permanently removed you from the loser category. Because you are a child of God, you already measure up. Christ is your sufficiency. He makes you "good enough" for any task that He calls you to do.

"Not that we are sufficient of ourselves to think of anything as being from ourselves, but our sufficiency is from God, who also made us sufficient as ministers of the new covenant, not of the letter but of the Spirit; for the letter kills, but the Spirit gives life" (2 Corinthians 3:5-6).

Our weakness is not a problem for God, it is an asset. When the apostle Paul was hampered by a thorn in his flesh, he pleaded with God three times to remove it. God didn't remove it but instead gave sufficient grace for Paul to deal with it. *"And He said to me, 'My grace is sufficient for you, for My strength is made perfect in weakness.' Therefore most gladly I will rather boast in my infirmities, that the power of Christ may rest upon me. Therefore I take pleasure in infirmities, in reproaches, in needs, in persecutions, in distresses, for Christ's sake. For when I am weak, then I am strong"* (2 Corinthians 12:9-10).

God does not require us to earn His approval by our own resources. To do so would make us vulnerable to sin. How? For those who see themselves as good enough, pride takes root and that is sin. The Pharisees did their righteousness on their own terms. They saw themselves as holy and despised others. Jesus wasn't impressed with this attitude or their self-righteous lifestyle.

On the other hand, the person who constantly sees himself as deficient and unworthy has the focus on himself and not on Christ. That, also, is sin. If I'm at the center of my world, then my world will be reduced to what I think I can do. Christ wants to be the center of my world. When Christ is at the center, I can do all things. When I am at the center, I can do nothing.

The individuals trying to do the Christian life by their own strength will also be vulnerable to being perfectionists. Perfectionism is a response to a fear of failure that focuses on what I must do in my own strength and ability and leaves God out of the process. We attempt to do things *for* God instead of allowing Him to work His will *through* us. Although we wouldn't outright admit it, we don't want His help. We do not want to be dependent on grace but rather desire to show Jesus a perfect finished product. Perfectionism actually makes us separate from Christ, rather than enhancing the relationship, because we don't draw near for His filling and enablement.

When we have low self-esteem, we can also be controlled by what we think other people think about us. This is a subtle trap that can elevate the opinions of others above the opinion of God. In trying to please everyone else, we invariably end up not being obedient to Jesus. *"The fear of man brings a snare, but whoever trusts in the LORD shall be safe"(Proverbs 29:25).*

Fear is a powerful emotion – it can cause us to do all sorts of things that we otherwise wouldn't do. Fear can drive us to jump to conclusions about God and His motives. The more we give in to fear, it seems, the less we trust His attentiveness, His concern, His love, and His power.

In Numbers chapter 13 and 14, we have the historical account of the Israelites on the border of the Promised Land that God desired to give them. Twelve men were sent in to get a look at what kind of land it was. All twelve men admitted that the land was good, but ten of them were frightened by the size of the inhabitants. They gave a bad report about the land and persuaded the people to fear. The nation of Israel feared the enemy more than they feared their God. They refused to obey Him and take the land that He had prepared for them. Fear snuffed out their faith and kept them from God's plan for their lives. Fear nullified the promises of God in their hearts. They forgot that it was the God who called them that would also equip them.

What was God's response to their fear? Was He sympathetic and willing to let them out of the assignment He had given them because He felt sorry for them? No way. He was angry. *"Then the LORD said to Moses: 'How long will these people reject Me? And how long will they not believe Me, with all the signs which I have performed among them?'"* (Numbers 14:11). He equated their fear with rejection, unbelief, and infidelity. Being afraid was not a good enough reason for disobedience.

So how do we combat feelings of being inadequate? We learned in the previous chapter that God is for us, so the best place to turn when you feel overwhelmed with feelings of inadequacy is to Him. *"From the end of the earth I will cry to You, when my heart is overwhelmed; lead me to the rock that is higher than I" (Psalm 61:2).* Claim your status as a child of God indwelt by the Holy Spirit who is actively working in your life.

Walk by the Holy Spirit and counteract Satan's lies with the truth of your relationship to Christ. Refuse to give weight to the self-condemning thoughts. You have been redeemed.

In Matthew 14:24-33, we read the account of Peter walking on the water. The disciples were in a boat in the middle of the night, and the sea was rough because of a stiff wind. Jesus had been praying alone on the mountain and then He came to them, walking on the churning sea. The men were frightened, thinking they were seeing a ghost. But Jesus called out and reassured them that it was truly Him.

Peter is watching Jesus and he's thinking that it would be cool to walk on water with Jesus. And so he asks Jesus to command him to get out of the boat. Jesus says, "Come" and Peter is totally focused on Christ. He gets down out of the boat and walks toward Jesus. He really does it. He's walking on the water.

But then he starts to look around and he sees the choppy sea and feels the boisterous wind and suddenly his attention is not on the powerful Christ but on the powerful storm. Verse 30 says that *"he was afraid"* and then he began to sink.

The very same thing happens to us. When we start focusing on our difficulties or our own lack of self-worth instead of on Christ, fear kicks in and we begin to sink emotionally.

But Peter got it right. As soon as he began to sink he cried out to the Lord and *"immediately Jesus stretched out His hand and caught him."*

Perhaps you think, because you can't see God working in your life, that He isn't. But there is more going on than you realize. You are not omniscient. God IS working – all the time.

God's mercies are new every morning. We get a fresh supply of grace with the start of each new day. *"Through the LORD'S mercies we are not consumed, because His compassions fail not. They are new every morning; great is Your faithfulness"* (Lamentations 3:22-23).

Yesterday's failures are cleansed away and each day is a clean slate. The sins and mistakes of the day before, if confessed to God, are wiped

> *God's mercies are new every morning. We get a fresh supply of grace with the start of each new day.*

away. When God was training the nation of Israel in the wilderness to be His people, He instructed them to collect the manna every morning. When they tried to keep some of the manna for the next day, it developed worms and smelled bad. Why did God do it that way? I think He wanted to train the Israelites to be dependent on Him every day. Each morning, when they went out to collect their day's allotment of manna, they would find fresh evidence that God was still in their midst and caring for their needs. Especially after they blew it by being too fearful to go into the Promised

Land, they might have thought that God would abandon them. But the manna every morning and the pillar of cloud during the day and fire at night were daily evidence that God was still there.

God abundantly pardons and chooses to remember our sins no more. He extends fresh mercy to us each new day. God never calls us losers, never gives up on us, never writes us off as hopeless cases. When we stumble and fall, God picks us up with compassion. *"Therefore we do not lose heart. Even though our outward man is perishing, yet the inward man is being renewed day by day" (2 Corinthians 4:16).*

21

The Danger of Comparison

"Stand fast therefore in the liberty by which Christ has made us free, and do not be entangled again with a yoke of bondage" (Galatians 5:1).

How prone we are to compare ourselves with others. We compare in an effort to reassure ourselves of our own value, yet the exercise does more to produce bondage than to relieve our anxiety. We torment ourselves with thoughts that we aren't as good or aren't as blessed as someone else. We compare in a desperate hope that we won't be deemed a failure, and yet it leads us down a path of sin that can itself make our lives ineffective for God unless the comparison prompts us to change.

If we compare ourselves with someone who is more mature in Christ and it provokes us to grow, that is a good thing. Paul, in writing to the Corinthians, urges the believers to *"imitate me, just as I imitate Christ."* The writer of Hebrews declares, *"And we desire that each one of you show the same diligence to the full assurance of hope until the end, that you do not become sluggish, but imitate those who through faith and patience inherit the promises"* (Hebrews 6:11-12). For many of us, it helps to have a visual aid of how to live the Christian life.

But whenever our sizing up of ourselves in relation to others produces envy, jealousy, inferiority, or pride, that is when comparisons become counterproductive.

We compare ourselves with others and chase the contentment that we think would come if we knew we were on par with our peers. But rarely do we see ourselves as equal to others. Most of the time we make winners and losers.

"For we dare not class ourselves or compare ourselves with those who commend themselves. But they, measuring themselves by themselves, and comparing themselves among themselves, are not wise…But 'he who glories, let him glory in the Lord.' For not he who commends himself is approved, but whom the Lord commends" (2 Corinthians 10:12, 17-18).

When we compare ourselves with others, what questions are we really trying to answer? Something in our soul wants to know: "Am I good enough? Do I measure up? Am I worthy of love or respect? Is God pleased with me?" Often we think that God loves someone else more than He loves us because that person's life seems to be going better than ours.

But those questions aren't answered by comparing ourselves with others. God has a yardstick all His own. Humans look at numbers or influence or name recognition or opportunities to do something big. God doesn't do that. When He evaluates His children, He wants to know: "Did she obey Me? Did his character represent Me well? Did she glorify Me?"

Comparisons are not usually based on reality. We look at the most successful thing in someone else's life and judge them as worthy. But when we look at ourselves, we only look at our failures and shortcomings. It's not a fair comparison. Often we compare ourselves with cultural "shoulds." We tell ourselves, "by this age I should be married, I should have a fulfilling career, I should have my own house." I should. I should. I should. There is no way to win against such thinking.

"But as for me, my feet had almost stumbled; my steps had nearly slipped. For I was envious of the boastful, when I saw the prosperity of the wicked" (Psalm 73:2-3).

Comparisons often end in envy and jealousy. In God's eyes, envy is not harmless. *"But if you have bitter envy and self-seeking in your hearts, do not boast and lie against the truth. This wisdom does not descend from above, but is earthly, sensual, demonic. For where envy and self-seeking exist, confusion and every evil thing are there. But the wisdom that is from above is first pure, then peaceable, gentle, willing to yield, full of mercy and good fruits, without partiality and without hypocrisy" (James 3:14-17).*

James calls envy *"earthly, sensual, and demonic."* Saul was king over the nation of Israel – a man of power and position. Yet he fell victim to the trap of comparison. After 40 days of stalemate between the forces of the Philistines and the forces of Saul, an unknown young man named David killed the giant named Goliath. During the ensuing battle, the Israelites thoroughly routed the Philistines and there was a great victory. King Saul should have been praising God for deliverance from the Philistine problem, but instead he was caught up in his own insecurities.

"Now it had happened as they were coming home, when David was returning from the slaughter of the Philistine, that the women had come out of all the cities of Israel, singing and dancing, to meet King Saul, with tambourines, with joy, and with musical instruments. So the women sang as they danced, and said: 'Saul has slain his thousands, and David his ten thousands.' Then Saul was very angry, and the saying displeased him; and he said, 'They have ascribed to David ten thousands, and to me they have ascribed only thousands. Now what more can he have but the kingdom?' So Saul eyed David from that day forward. And it happened on the next day that the distressing spirit from God came upon Saul, and he prophesied inside the house. So David played music with his hand, as at other times; but there was a spear in Saul's hand. And Saul cast the spear, for he said, 'I will pin David to the wall!' But David escaped his presence twice. Now Saul was afraid of David, because the LORD was with him, but had departed from Saul" (1 Samuel 18:6-12).

Saul spent the rest of his reign as king being jealous of David and relentlessly hunting him in an effort to kill him. The habit of comparing ourselves with others is destructive and puts a person in bondage.

Those prone to the comparison game can be discontent and may even blame God for not blessing them as He has "obviously" blessed someone else. Or they may refuse to serve the Lord, as Moses did at the burning bush, because of a sense of inadequacy. If you refer back to that passage in Exodus chapter 3, you'll see that God wasn't at all pleased with Moses' attitude. To God it was disobedience. God countered Moses' objections with the declaration of His Presence. When Moses still gave excuses, God got angry.

Barnabas is a Christian who seemed not to get trapped in comparisons or insecurities. His given name was Joses, but the Christians called him Barnabas which means "Son of Encouragement." Barnabas was a wealthy, influential Christian in the early church who was filled with the Holy Spirit and faith. When Saul of Tarsus was newly saved, the brothers in Jerusalem didn't want to have anything to do with him because they didn't believe that he had become a disciple. It was Barnabas that convinced the church that Saul was a genuine believer.

When the church in Antioch began to grow rapidly, the Jerusalem church sent Barnabas to go and help lead the believers in Antioch. Barnabas was a good man who could see the grace of God working in people that other Christians might not have wanted to trust. Wherever he saw God at work, he rejoiced. While at Antioch, Barnabas went in search of Saul because he knew his friend had gifts that would benefit the new believers in Antioch. Then, when the church determined to send them out to share the gospel in other regions, Barnabas and Saul formed a team. At first the references to the team were "Barnabas and Saul." After they left the island of Cyprus, however, it became *"Paul and his party."* From that point on, Paul was the main speaker and Barnabas played the backup role (except when they traveled to Jerusalem). There is no evidence that Barnabas had a problem with turning the leadership over to Paul. Barnabas saw the value and potential in others and was secure enough in himself that he didn't need to compare and compete.

"For if anyone thinks himself to be something, when he is nothing, he deceives himself. But let each one examine his own work, and then he will have rejoicing in himself alone, and not in another" (Galatians 6:4).

In this way, Barnabas imitated Jesus. In the passage of Scripture where Jesus washes the feet of the disciples, it is said that *"Jesus, knowing that the Father had given all things into His hands, and that He had come from God and was going to God, rose from supper and laid aside His garments, took a towel and girded Himself. After that, He poured water into a basin and began to wash the disciples' feet, and to wipe them with the towel with which He was girded"* (John 13:3-5). Jesus knew who He was, and so He could take a lowly position and minister to His disciples.

Jesus and Barnabas knew that the glory and work of God was more important than their own status. They could be humble without selfish ambition. They did not need to maintain a certain prestige.

That is not to say that Barnabas was a pushover. Later, when they determined to revisit the churches that they had started, Barnabas was determined to take Mark, who had fallen short the first time around and left the work. Paul was just as determined that Mark would not go. But

Barnabas didn't back down. Mark's future usefulness was too important. So Barnabas and Paul split up and formed two missionary teams. That trip was instrumental in restoring Mark to trustworthiness. After that trip, God used Mark to write one of the four gospels in our Bible. Mark's initial failure was turned around by a man named Barnabas who was secure enough in himself to go to bat for the guy that others thought should be shunned.

How can we overcome the tendency to compare ourselves with others? First off, like Barnabas, we need to be full of the Holy Spirit. When we walk with the Spirit, God's glory will be far more important to us than our own. We will be secure in the knowledge that God loves us and values us by a different standard than the world's. We need to affirm who we are in Christ and train ourselves as an act of our will to see ourselves as God sees us and not as we see ourselves.

"Let a man so consider us, as servants of Christ and stewards of the mysteries of God. Moreover it is required in stewards that one be found faithful. But with me it is a very small thing that I should be judged by you or by a human court. In fact, I do not even judge myself. For I know nothing against myself, yet I am not justified by this; but He who judges me is the Lord. Therefore judge nothing before the time, until the Lord comes, who will both bring to light the hidden things of darkness and reveal the counsels of the hearts. Then each one's praise will come from God. Now these things, brethren, I have figuratively transferred to myself and Apollos for your sakes, that you may learn in us not to think beyond what is written, that none of you may be puffed up on behalf of one against the other. For who makes you differ from another? And what do you have that you did not receive? Now if you did indeed receive it, why do you boast as if you had not received it?" (1 Corinthians 4:1-7).

Understand that the habit of comparison – if it leads to envy, jealousy, an inferiority complex, or pride – is destructive and offensive to God. *"A sound heart is life to the body, but envy is rottenness to the bones" (Proverbs 14:30).*

We need to deliberately guard ourselves from comparing ourselves with others and also to guard against setting up others to make comparisons. *"If we live in the Spirit, let us also walk in the Spirit. Let us not become conceited, provoking one another, envying one another" (Galatians 5:25-26).*

After Jesus' resurrection, Peter and Jesus have a conversation about Peter's future. Peter sees John and asks Jesus, "What about this man?" Jesus says, "What is that to you? You follow Me." Jesus wasn't about to let

Peter start comparing himself to John. Each would have their own ministry. Each would be useful to God in his own way. And that would be enough. There would be no need to compare the two.

> *Refuse to consider your inadequacies and rather realize that weakness and dependence are huge strengths in God's eyes. Let God use you.*

Refuse to consider your inadequacies and rather realize that weakness and dependence are huge strengths in God's eyes. Let God use you.

Finally, as an act of your will, thank and praise God for how He is blessing and using others that you envy. Do not let His favor on them create a root of bitterness in your own heart. Do not let envy destroy the fellowship that you have with those other people. As you thank God for working in them, your heart will be softened toward them and perhaps your attitude will change. It's difficult to be miffed about an answer to your own prayer. Regardless, God will be glorified and you will be kept from sin and that is what is most important.

"But above all these things put on love, which is the bond of perfection. And let the peace of God rule in your hearts, to which also you were called in one body; and be thankful" (Colossians 3:14-15).

22

Not Controlled by Circumstances

"For we walk by faith, not by sight" (2 Corinthians 5:7).

Asa, king of Judah, was generally a good king, especially in his younger years. Because he relied on the Lord, his armies were able to defeat much stronger and larger armies. But later in life, his adversary, the king of Israel, began to fortify cities on the border of Judah. Asa looked at the circumstances and decided that he needed to pay off the king of neighboring Syria to stop the king of Israel. He did not rely on the Lord but implemented his own solution to the threat.

Abraham looked to the slave woman Hagar to give him a son instead of to his wife because he and Sarah looked at their circumstances and concluded that God needed a little help to provide Abraham an heir and fulfill His promise of a mighty nation from the seed of Abraham.

The Israelites refused to take the land which God had promised them because there were giants in the land. The circumstances, they believed, didn't look good; they were afraid that they would be wiped out. All these failures of faith came about because the participants considered what they could see as more real than the promises of God.

But the circumstances that we see with our eyes are not the whole reality that exists, especially for people of faith. As humans, we are not all-knowing or all-seeing. But our God is. And yet we sometimes behave as though the reverse is true. In my spiritual youth, I judged almost everything by circumstances, looking for signs to confirm a decision rather than trusting the Scriptures. I was much like the double-minded man of James chapter one – like a wave of the sea driven and tossed by the wind, unstable in all my ways.

Focusing on our circumstances and what we can see is the opposite of faith.

Focusing on our circumstances and what we can see is the opposite of faith. *"Now faith is the substance of things hoped for, the evidence of things not seen"* (Hebrews 11:1). When we focus on our circumstances and trust solely in our perception of reality, we are eliminating God and anything supernatural from the equation. We bring everything down to a purely human level and walk by sight and not by faith.

"But without faith it is impossible to please Him, for he who comes to God must believe that He is, and that He is a rewarder of those who diligently seek Him" (Hebrews 11:6).

Allowing our emotions to be controlled by our circumstances in effect characterizes God as impotent or uncaring (or both). And yet our faithful God is neither. He is ready to bring His abundant and sufficient resources to bear when we respond in faith to a situation.

In Old Testament history, God thwarted the Syrian army by informing the prophet Elisha of the Syrian king's plans. Elisha then relayed that information to King Jehoram and the Israeli army by telling them where the king of Syria was going to set ambushes. The king of Syria became increasingly frustrated with the failure of his military efforts, so he determined to send an army to capture Elisha and get rid of the supernatural informant.

"Therefore he sent horses and chariots and a great army there, and they came by night and surrounded the city. And when the servant of the man of God arose early and went out, there was an army, surrounding the city with

horses and chariots. And his servant said to him, 'Alas, my master! What shall we do?'" (2 Kings 6:14-15).

Looking at the circumstances, Elisha and his servant were in an extremely precarious position. Their heads were about to roll. And yet, Elisha wasn't sweating. He was confident in an overwhelming situation because his faith was secure in El Shaddai – the Almighty God.

"So he answered, 'Do not fear, for those who are with us are more than those who are with them.' And Elisha prayed, and said, 'LORD, I pray, open his eyes that he may see.' Then the LORD opened the eyes of the young man, and he saw. And behold, the mountain was full of horses and chariots of fire all around Elisha" (2 Kings 6:16-17).

Not long ago, God showed me His power over circumstances. Our campus ministry group, Campus Bible Fellowship, was doing an overnight retreat at a state park. As part of the event we had a campfire on Friday night. Because of chemical sensitivities, campfire smoke is usually a really bad substance for me. It causes coughing, huge pain, a headache, and mental fogginess. I can be sick for days. But that didn't cross my mind as I built the fire because I had no reaction to the smoke. I just sort of forgot that I wasn't supposed to be able to sit around a campfire for several hours.

Then the men and I stayed up late talking about God and the things of faith and life. It was a tremendous conversation that I thoroughly enjoyed. At 4 a.m. we decided to turn in. I set the alarm for 7:30 a.m. so that I could make breakfast for the group. But the caffeine in the soda that we were drinking kept me awake until 5 a.m. The thought briefly went through my head that I was in big trouble. I am a woman with fibromyalgia who doesn't do well without an adequate amount of sleep. There was no possible way for me to function well that day. The circumstances did not look good. But God was continuing to do something miraculous.

I awoke without an alarm at 7:15 a.m. I felt completely refreshed. So I got up and began the day with no fatigue. Later I built a fire and cooked lunch over the fire – again with no reaction to the smoke. I forgot that I'm not supposed to be able to do that. It was amazing – for more than 30 hours I was invincible. It was a direct intervention of God. God has the ability and the authority to overrule the natural order of things because they are His laws.

"For whatever is born of God overcomes the world. And this is the victory that has overcome the world-- our faith" (1 John 5:4).

And that's the point. God is intervening in our lives all the time. So we need to operate in faith rather than strictly by looking at our circumstances. We need to focus on what God has promised and on His character rather than on the circumstances that we perceive. Our understanding of the past and present is quite limited, and our understanding of the future is nil. So why would we judge God by what we see rather than by what He has declared in the Bible? Will God ever be a liar?

> *God is intervening in our lives all the time. So we need to operate in faith rather than strictly by looking at our circumstances.*

"Thus God, determining to show more abundantly to the heirs of promise the immutability of His counsel, confirmed it by an oath, that by two immutable things, in which it is impossible for God to lie, we might have strong consolation, who have fled for refuge to lay hold of the hope set before us. This hope we have as an anchor of the soul, both sure and steadfast, and which enters the Presence behind the veil, where the forerunner has entered for us, even Jesus, having become High Priest forever according to the order of Melchizedek "(Hebrews 6:17-20).

In the Christian life, contentment cannot rely on circumstances because circumstances are constantly changing. The events in our lives are temporary, but our relationship with God is eternal. You and I can be content despite the difficulties in our lives because God is faithful to us in the midst of those difficulties.

"Let your conduct be without covetousness; be content with such things as you have. For He Himself has said, 'I will never leave you nor forsake you.' So we may boldly say: 'The Lord is my helper; I will not fear. What can man do to me?'" (Hebrews 13:5-6).

God's worthiness and righteousness is in no way dependent on what is going on down here on earth. Our situation doesn't change the character of God. It is impossible for our constantly changing circumstances to define an unchanging, transcendent God. The Lord remains the same – perfect in all His attributes. The Lord is righteous; He is good and perfect and without mistake.

God desires that I delight in His will – not merely endure it or grudgingly submit to it. We don't delight in pain, but we delight in His Presence and in realizing that we are part of something bigger than ourselves.

"Now thanks be to God who always leads us in triumph in Christ, and through us diffuses the fragrance of His knowledge in every place. For we are to God the fragrance of Christ among those who are being saved and among those who are perishing. To the one we are the aroma of death leading to death, and to the other the aroma of life leading to life. And who is sufficient for these things?" (2 Corinthians 2:14-16).

Anyone can be sweet when the conditions are good; there is nothing supernatural about that. It doesn't take Jesus or faith. But when the situation is adverse and we remain patient, kind, and self-controlled, it shows the power of Christ in our lives. Our behavior *"adorns the doctrine of God our Savior in all things."*

Therefore, every day is a good day for a Christian. I cannot judge a day by my feelings or by circumstances. Every day is a good day because God has made it; God is in it, and God has not changed His promises in the last 24 hours. His goodness and mercy are still following me. God is the ultimate ruler and architect over the day. Who am I to give a bad rating to a day that the Lord has made and thereby justify my unrighteous attitude?

"This is the day the LORD has made; we will rejoice and be glad in it" *(Psalm 118:24).* On easy days I require the grace of God, and on hard days, His grace is sufficient. God remains the same. My attitude needs to be one of trust in sunshine and in rain.

Grouching about circumstances doesn't reflect well on Jesus if we look at Him as the One who is ultimately controlling the events of our lives. If God is ultimately sovereign, then if I complain I am complaining against Him. I am, in effect, saying that Christ isn't doing a very good job with my life. And that destroys hope.

"And not only that, but we also glory in tribulations, knowing that tribulation produces perseverance; and perseverance, character; and character, hope. Now hope does not disappoint, because the love of God has been poured out in our hearts by the Holy Spirit who was given to us" (Romans 5:3-5).

Yes, it is harder to walk by faith when sight seems to contradict. But the Scriptures are reality. In a storm, a pilot needs to fly by the instruments, not by what he sees before him. Such also is the walk of faith. I cannot rely on my own understanding. It is faulty. My perceptions will tell me that

I'm without hope, but that is not accurate. I need to fly by the instruments, trusting that what the Scriptures declare will be true in my life as well. The Lord will pull it together as He sees best.

We maintain spiritual equilibrium by refusing to judge God, His work, or ourselves on the basis of feelings and circumstances. *"For the weapons of our warfare are not carnal but mighty in God for pulling down strongholds, casting down arguments and every high thing that exalts itself against the knowledge of God, bringing every thought into captivity to the obedience of Christ" (2 Corinthians 10:4-5).*

Contemplating Jesus will keep me from contemplating my own weaknesses and the enormity of the difficulties. If we focus too much on the obstacles, they will crush us. Contemplating Christ gives us peace.

23

A Lifestyle of Worship

"Oh come, let us worship and bow down; let us kneel before the LORD our Maker. For He is our God, and we are the people of His pasture, and the sheep of His hand" (Psalm 95:6-7).

In this book, we have seen the excellencies of the Holy Spirit and the tremendous provisions that our God has made for His children. Those that have received Jesus Christ as their Savior have been elevated from the position of enemy and rebel to the position of precious, beloved child of God and joint heir with Christ.

The Holy Spirit infuses our lives with His character, He gives us victory over sin, He comforts, guides, teaches, protects, strengthens, and equips us for service. He satisfies our souls.

We are in all ways blessed and provided for. That should produce in us a white-hot desire to worship Him who has done so much for us.

He rescues us from our lies. We are in all ways blessed and provided for. That should produce in us a white-hot desire to worship Him who has done so much for us.

"Bless the LORD, O my soul; and all that is within me, bless His holy name!" (Psalm 103:1) Our entire life should be an act of worship in response to what our God has done for us.

"I beseech you therefore, brethren, by the mercies of God, that you present your bodies a living sacrifice, holy, acceptable to God, which is your reasonable service. And do not be conformed to this world, but be transformed by the renewing of your mind, that you may prove what is that good and acceptable and perfect will of God" (Romans 12:1-2).

As followers of Christ, we are called to be living sacrifices as an act of worship of the One who loved us and gave Himself for us. Worship that honors God goes far beyond singing a set of songs on Sunday morning.

Worship must be a lifestyle involving everything we think, everything we do, and everything we are. The worship that we are called to – what the apostle Paul calls our "reasonable service" – is a complete surrender of our sovereignty to the Lord Jesus Christ.

"I have been crucified with Christ; it is no longer I who live, but Christ lives in me; and the life which I now live in the flesh I live by faith in the Son of God, who loved me and gave Himself for me. I do not set aside the grace of God; for if righteousness comes through the law, then Christ died in vain" (Galatians 2:20-21).

In the hour of worship, only God is great. It's all about God's magnificence, God's power, God's graciousness, God's amazing love. Worship is all about God – not about us.

In the hour of worship, only God is great. It's all about God's magnificence, God's power, God's graciousness, God's amazing love. Worship is all about God – not about us. If God is not the focal point, it isn't biblical worship.

When I lived in Russia, I had a blonde, fuzzy-faced little dog named Sonia who was a good picture of what it is to worship a master. We had a game we played when I came home each day. She'd be sitting in the windowsill looking out the window and watching for me. As I approached the building I would wave and her whole being would respond. Her ears would perk up and her little body would start to quiver. As soon as I entered the building to go up to our third floor apartment, she would leap off the windowsill and rush to the door. When I walked in she would greet me, jumping up and down and kissing my face in total delight that I was home. A greeting like that dispelled whatever bad day that I might have been having. She worshipped me and she unashamedly declared her love for me every time I came in the door.

Are we that delighted to come into the Presence of the Lord? Are we waiting for His wave so that we can run to meet Him and adore Him? *"And you shall love the Lord your God with all your heart, with all your soul, with all your mind, and with all your strength"* (Mark 12:30).

The most frequently used word for worship in the Hebrew language of the Old Testament is "shachah" which means to make oneself bow or kneel down in humility or adoration. It means to get down on your belly before God. Although we can't go through our day with our face on the floor, we should be bowed down in our heart before God - yielding to Him His true position. *"Give to the LORD the glory due His name; bring an offering, and come before Him. Oh, worship the LORD in the beauty of holiness!"* (1 Chronicles 16:29).

Worship is to declare God the ruler and myself the follower. It is to affirm the greatness of God and the littleness of me before Him. It is to say, "Yes, Lord!" and then ask, "What's the question?"

The worship that God delights in will be worship that has been guided by the Holy Spirit. *"But the hour is coming, and now is, when the true worshipers will worship the Father in spirit and truth; for the Father is seeking such to worship Him. God is Spirit, and those who worship Him must worship in spirit and truth"* (John 4:23-24).

The Spirit guides us moment by moment as worshippers in the world. We need Him to help us understand what would bring glory to God. A lot of what people call worship is really what we prefer rather than what would bring glory to God.

Walking by the Spirit is a much higher and more demanding calling than following a set of rules. *"These people draw near to Me with their mouth, and honor Me with their lips, but their heart is far from Me. And in vain they worship Me, teaching as doctrines the commandments of men"* (Matthew 15:8-9).

Jesus wants us to have a relationship with Himself. He wants to set us free from man-imposed rules and make us truly righteous from the inside out by the power of the Holy Spirit. Following Christ by the direction of the Holy Spirit is supernatural, not natural. We can be mediocre in our own strength but truly exceptional by the power of God because Christ's strength is sufficient for all that He calls us to do.

Humility is the essence of worship. We ascribe worth to God when we obey Him. We have seen His brilliance, His power, His holiness. We have seen how far below that standard we are. Humility before God is the only response that makes sense. And when we see that all the best stuff in us is a gift from God, we will not lord it over our fellow human beings. By the grace we have been given in Christ, we can extend grace to others and treat their needs as more important than our own.

In humility we look to obey our Lord in every respect with every fiber of our being. *"If you love Me, keep My commandments" (John 14:15).* We walk daily by the power of the Holy Spirit in an attitude of absolute dependence before God. Obedience to God becomes worship because we are taking Him at His word and declaring Him worthy to direct our lives.

Our worship should go beyond Sunday and fill Monday through Saturday. Everything we do can be an act of worship. *"For the love of Christ compels us, because we judge thus: that if One died for all, then all died; and He died for all, that those who live should live no longer for themselves, but for Him who died for them and rose again" (2 Corinthians 5:14-15).*

We are cheerful when we want to complain because we follow Jesus and want to honor Him. We engage in our business dealings with honor and integrity because we love the Lord. *"And whatever you do, do it heartily, as to the Lord and not to men, knowing that from the Lord you will receive the reward of the inheritance; for you serve the Lord Christ" (Colossians 3:23-24).*

We tell the truth and avoid even the hint of deception because we want to represent Christ well in our world. A lifestyle of worship means that if we can't do something to the glory of God, we ought not engage in that activity.

"Therefore, whether you eat or drink, or whatever you do, do all to the glory of God. Give no offense, either to the Jews or to the Greeks or to the church of God, just as I also please all men in all things, not seeking my own profit, but the profit of many, that they may be saved" (1 Corinthians 10:31-33).

It is worship when we train ourselves to consistently have a vertical focus and include Jesus in our dealings and decisions throughout the day. As we face situations in our day, we silently ask Him for wisdom. Although some would suggest that such a stance is using God as a crutch for the weak, in reality it is far from weakness. It is no more weakness than a soldier diligently following the instructions of his commanding officer. We harness our strength and submit it to Jesus Christ to bring glory to God. The soldier who does his own thing and disregards his orders dishonors his commander and his unit and puts their lives in danger.

When we feel overwhelmed or sad or angry or afraid, we can turn to Jesus for help in conquering our emotions and leveraging our strengths. When we refuse to fear and worry when we face trials, when we live as though the Bible is true, when we trust Him and walk in faith – then we are worshipping.

"Oh come, let us sing to the LORD! Let us shout joyfully to the Rock of our salvation. Let us come before His presence with thanksgiving; let us shout joyfully to Him with psalms. For the LORD is the great God, and the great King above all gods" (Psalm 95:1-3).

CPSIA information can be obtained at www.ICGtesting.com
Printed in the USA
BVOW08s1512180114

342192BV00002B/9/P